LENT
for
EVERYONE

MARK

YEAR B

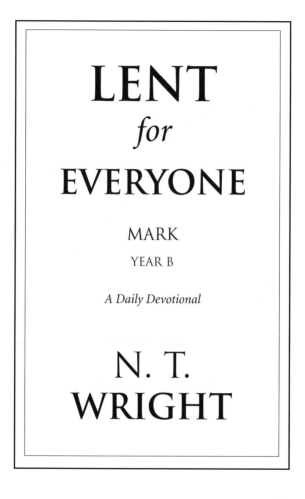

LENT
for
EVERYONE

MARK

YEAR B

A Daily Devotional

N. T.
WRIGHT

WJK WESTMINSTER
JOHN KNOX PRESS
LOUISVILLE • KENTUCKY

Copyright © Nicholas Thomas Wright 2012

Originally published in Great Britain in 2012 by
Society for Promoting Christian Knowledge

First published in the United States of America in 2012 by
Westminster John Knox Press

12 13 14 15 16 17 18 19 20 21—10 9 8 7 6 5 4 3 2 1

New Testament quotations are taken from The New Testament for Everyone series by
N. T. Wright, copyright © Nicholas Thomas Wright 2001–2011.
The extracts from the Old Testament are from the New Revised Standard Version of the Bible,
Anglicized Edition, copyright © 1989, 1995 by the Division of Christian Education
of the National Council of the Churches of Christ in the USA;
used by permission; all rights reserved.
Old Testament quotations marked NIV are from The Holy Bible, *New International Version*,
copyright © 1973, 1978, 1984 by the International Bible Society. Used by permission
of Zondervan Publishing House, with all rights reserved.

Extracts from hymns and worship songs appear on the following pages:
p. 85, 'In Christ alone' by Keith Getty and Stuart Townend.
Copyright © 2001 Kingsway Thankyou Music.
p. 115, 'Shine, Jesus, shine' by Graham Kendrick. Copyright © 1987 Make Way Music,
www.grahamkendrick.co.uk.
p. 154, 'Jesus is Lord!' by David J. Mansell. Copyright © 1982 Word's Spirit of Praise Music.
p. 159, 'Servant King' by Graham Kendrick. Copyright © 1983 Thankyou Music/PRS.

Cover design by Dilu Nicholas
Cover artwork by Sergiy Shkanov, Beginning, *oil and acrylic on canvas, 2008*

Library of Congress Cataloging-in-Publication Data is on file at the Library of
Congress, Washington, DC.

ISBN: 978–0–664–23894–0

PRINTED IN THE UNITED STATES OF AMERICA

♾ The paper used in this publication meets the minimum requirements of
the American National Standard for Information Sciences—Permanence
of Paper for Printed Library Materials, ANSI Z39.48-1992.

Westminster John Knox Press advocates the responsible use of our natural resources.
The text paper of this book is made from 30% postconsumer waste.

Most Westminster John Knox Press books are available at special quantity discounts when
purchased in bulk by corporations, organizations, and special-interest groups.
For more information, please e-mail SpecialSales@wjkbooks.com.

For

Ian, Stuart and Nick
faithful pastors, wise friends

CONTENTS

———➤•◊•◄———

Contents

ASH WEDNESDAY

Mark 1.1–20; focused on 1.1–9

¹This is where the good news starts – the good news of Jesus the Messiah, God's son.

²Isaiah the prophet put it like this ('Look! I am sending my messenger ahead of me; he will clear the way for you!'):

³'A shout goes up in the desert: Make way for the Lord! Clear a straight path for him!'

⁴John the Baptizer appeared in the desert. He was announcing a baptism of repentance, to forgive sins. ⁵The whole of Judaea, and everyone who lived in Jerusalem, went out to him; they confessed their sins and were baptized by him in the river Jordan. ⁶John wore camel-hair clothes, with a leather belt round his waist. He used to eat locusts and wild honey.

⁷'Someone a lot stronger than me is coming close behind,' John used to tell them. 'I don't deserve to squat down and undo his sandals. ⁸I've plunged you in the water; he's going to plunge you in the holy spirit.'

⁹This is how it happened. Around that time, Jesus came from Nazareth in Galilee, and was baptized by John in the river Jordan.

There was a man on the radio the other day enthusing about a new restaurant he'd just visited. Actually, he interviewed the chef, and got him to talk about the exciting new ingredients he was adding to his salads. Customers loved it, he said. The reporter hadn't been so keen to begin with, but gradually came round to the idea. The new, secret ingredient, mixed in with the lettuce and cucumber, was . . . locusts.

Well, explained the reporter cheerfully, you get used to prawns and other creatures with legs and eyes, don't you? And the taste (so he said) was really rather good. We shall have to see whether it catches on.

But I suspect that, even in the first century, the mention of someone, in this case John the Baptist, eating locusts was not meant to make people think, 'Good idea! Must try that some day.' Like the description of John's clothing, it was probably meant to highlight the fact that he appeared as a strange, wild man, living in a way that said, 'It's time for a change! Ordinary days are gone – a new age is just about to begin!'

That was the point, of course. We sometimes think of 'repentance' as being about going back: going back, wearily, to the place you went wrong, finally making a clean breast of it, and then hoping you can start again. Well, that may be how it feels sometimes, and Ash Wednesday is no bad time to face up to such a moment if it's got to be done. But John's message of repentance was essentially forward-looking. God's doing a new thing, so we have to get ready! If you suddenly got a phone call telling you that someone really important was coming to visit your house – the Queen, say, or even Victoria Beckham – you'd want to whip round the place with a duster, at least. Perhaps throw out that pile of magazines under the armchair. Maybe even do the left-over washing-up. Sort the place out, quick! She's on the way!

That is the mood John was evoking – and that's the mood Mark is creating in his characteristically breathless opening. 'This is where the good news starts': you can almost feel Mark being out of breath having run all the way up the road to your house. 'Good news!' (puff, pant). 'He's on the way!' (gasp, deep breath). 'Get ready now – he's nearly here!'

And who is this 'he' who is 'on the way'? Well, here's the puzzle which will occupy Mark, and us, throughout most of the book. Obviously, we say, it's Jesus: 'Jesus, the Messiah, God's son'. The phrase 'God's son' was used, in some key biblical passages, as a title for Israel's king. There are no signs in pre-Christian Judaism that it meant 'the second person of the Trinity'. Or that 'Messiah' meant anything like that, either. 'Messiah' meant 'the anointed one': again, pretty certainly a king.

But the two biblical passages Mark quotes (in his breathless state, he mentions Isaiah before quoting Malachi, and then comes back to Isaiah afterwards) – these two passages don't seem to be talking simply about a king, a human figure in the line of the monarchs of old. They seem to be talking about Israel's God himself. Malachi 3.1 talks of God sending a messenger ahead of him to get people ready. Isaiah 40.3 is clear as well. The person who's 'coming' is God himself!

Why? Wasn't God always, so to speak, 'there'? Why would he be 'coming'? Cut a long story very short: the ancient Jews believed that their God had abandoned Israel, and the Temple, at the time of the exile in Babylon, six centuries earlier. They had come back; they had rebuilt the Temple; but at no point did they have a sense that God had returned to live in it. (For a start, if he had, why were pagans still ruling over them?) So the great promises of God's return remained unfulfilled. And John the Baptist seemed to be saying that now was the time. He was on the way!

So Mark invites us, right off the top, to hold together two pictures. First, Israel's God is coming back at last! Second, here comes Jesus, Israel's true king, 'God's son' in that sense! How can we get our heads around that?

John doesn't give his hearers much time to think. He was plunging people into the river Jordan, but the Coming One – whoever he was – would plunge them in something much more dangerous and powerful. In the 'holy spirit'! That's another idea bursting in on Mark's hearers, making them wonder what on earth he's talking about. 'God's coming back! The Messiah's on the way! You'll be plunged in the spirit!' If you feel it's now your turn to be breathless, you're probably in good company. I suspect that his first readers felt the same.

But the point, of course – this is Ash Wednesday, after all – is that you need to get ready. When God arrives; when the king knocks on the door; when you're about to be plunged in the holy spirit – what is there in your life that most embarrasses you? What are you ashamed of? Which bits of the room have been quietly crying out to be tidied these many years, and you've been ignoring them? Mark is taking us on a pilgrimage this Lent, to the place where, he believes, God has come into our very midst – that is, to the cross of the Messiah. It's time to get ready.

Today

Wake us up, gracious Lord, by the message of your coming, and help us, in our hearts and our lives, to be ready.

THURSDAY AFTER ASH WEDNESDAY
Mark 1.21–45; focused on 1.21–28

[21]They went to Capernaum. At once, on the sabbath, Jesus went into the synagogue and taught. [22]They were astonished at his teaching. He wasn't like the legal teachers; he said things on his own authority.

[23]All at once, in their synagogue, there was a man with an unclean spirit.

[24]'What business have you got with us, Jesus of Nazareth?' he yelled. 'Have you come to destroy us? I know who you are: you're God's Holy One!'

[25]'Be quiet!' ordered Jesus. 'And come out of him!'

[26]The unclean spirit convulsed the man, gave a great shout, and came out of him. [27]Everyone was astonished.

'What's this?' they started to say to each other. 'New teaching – with real authority! He even tells the unclean spirits what to do, and they do it!'

[28]Word about Jesus spread at once, all over the surrounding district of Galilee.

It was the organist's night off. His deputy, fresh from college and looking even younger than he actually was, took charge of the choir. The singers – a good-hearted lot, but choirs will be choirs – were, almost instinctively, pushing the boundaries to see what would happen. Trivial things: a note fluffed here, a lead missed there. And – the most trivial of all, but a telltale sign of implicit rebellion – some were wearing brown shoes, not the regulation black.

I watched as they processed back after the service. The young man didn't bat an eyelid. Very quietly, but with deadly accuracy, he alerted them to the mistakes. 'And, gentlemen,' he added, 'black shoes, please.' He didn't raise his voice. He didn't need to. He was in charge, and they knew it. Point made. It was good to see.

The surprise of authority – someone's in charge here! We'd better sit up and take notice! – is what Mark is highlighting in this early incident in Jesus' public career. And it shows what so much of the gospel is all about. Jesus was going about telling people that God was at last becoming king. *And he was behaving as if he, himself, was in charge* – as if *he* were the king. There's the puzzle: as much a puzzle for Jesus' first hearers, and for Mark's as well, as it is for us.

Mark contrasts Jesus' authority with that of 'the legal teachers'. We may not immediately pick up the significance of that. In the modern Western world, 'legal teachers' would presumably be teaching in a law school, where young practitioners would be trained for their various tasks. But in ancient Israel a 'legal teacher' was much more than that.

Israel's 'law', after all, went back to Moses – or rather, to God himself, on Mount Sinai. The law, for them, wasn't just a system of rules and regulations. It was (so they believed) the ultimate revelation of what it meant to be human. What it meant to be God's people. And when the Jewish people were hemmed in and oppressed by pagan enemies – as they were in Jesus' day – the law was the badge they wore, proudly, to show that they really belonged to God even if things were tough just now. To 'teach the law' in that world was much more than training the next generation of barristers. It meant setting the social and cultural boundaries. It meant maintaining God's people in their distinct, and special, identity.

But the people who taught the law did so not on their own authority but by interpreting and applying existing law, both written and oral. 'This is what so-and-so taught,' they would say, quoting both recent and ancient authorities. But Jesus didn't do that. As we see in the other gospels (the Sermon on the Mount, for instance), he was quite outspoken. 'You've heard that it was said . . . but I say to you . . . !' He behaved, and spoke, as if he was in charge.

And he backed up his speaking with action. Here we run into a problem – for us. In Jesus' world, as in many parts of the world today (but not usually so visibly in the modern West), people's lives were blighted by forces or powers beyond their control, forces that seemed to take them over. People say, in our world, 'I don't know what made me do it.' People in Jesus' world reckoned they *did* know why some people seemed totally 'off the rails': there were hostile 'spiritual' forces out there, hard to define, but powerful in their effect. Calling such a force a 'demon' or an 'unclean spirit' doesn't mean they knew exactly what it was. It was a way of saying that the person was over-powered by an outside force. A malign power from beyond themselves.

And part of the point of God becoming king at last, which was the centre of the message of Jesus, was that all rival powers were being defeated. Jesus came with power and authority greater than the forces that had corrupted and defaced human lives. For God to become king meant that all other forces had to be dethroned. And the most obvious sign of that was that the dark, shadowy forces that had seized control of some benighted individuals were being decisively challenged.

These 'forces' were cunning. They seemed to know too much. Here and elsewhere we see the people they controlled shouting out what Jesus wanted at that stage to keep secret. He was God's Holy One (verse 24); and he had come, ultimately, to destroy all forces of evil in the world. They seemed to have an 'inside track' on spiritual realities. (Whether we moderns like it or not, by the way, this is a sure sign that stories like this weren't made up. The early Christians were unlikely to invent 'testimony' to Jesus from the lips of highly disturbed individuals.)

For Mark, and I suggest for us, stories like this should flag up the fact that there are many things in the world that appear to go horribly wrong which the best brains we have can't even analyse, let alone solve. The experience of terrifying and inhumane regimes around the world over the last century teaches us that forces can be unleashed which make people do unimaginably terrible things to one another. And all this has happened at a time when, in the modern Western world at least, people have banished 'religion', and even Jesus, to the sidelines, into the corner labelled 'personal therapy and lifestyle'.

Fortunately, Jesus refuses to stay in such a corner – just as he refused to fit into the expectations of the townsfolk at Capernaum. He insists on being in charge, even though it will be at the cost of his own life. That is the pattern of the whole gospel, ending up on the cross itself where, strangely, Jesus defeats all the powers of darkness.

Today

Sovereign Lord, help us to trust you when things seem out of control.

FRIDAY AFTER ASH WEDNESDAY

Mark 2.1–17; focused on 2.13–17

[13]Once more Jesus went out beside the sea. All the crowd came to him, and he taught them.

[14]As he went along he saw Levi, son of Alphaeus, sitting at the toll booth. 'Follow me!' he said. And he got up and followed him.

[15]That's how Jesus came to be sitting at home with lots of tax-collectors and sinners. There they were, plenty of them, sitting with Jesus and his disciples; they had become his followers.

> [16]When the legal experts from the Pharisees saw him eating
> with tax-collectors and sinners, they said to his disciples, 'Why
> does he eat with tax-collectors and sinners?'
> [17]When Jesus heard it, he said to them, 'It's sick people
> who need the doctor, not healthy ones. I came to call the bad
> people, not the good ones.'

Three times yesterday the doorbell rang unexpectedly. First
it was the engineer; he came to inspect the foundations of
the outhouse. Then it was the builder; he came to measure
for some windows that need replacing. Finally it was the
electrician; he came to fix some damaged light fittings. (Like
the mythical Number 17 bus: you wait for ages, and then three
come at the same time.) They came, each of them, to do a job.
All went off happily with the job done.

Perhaps the most interesting word in this fascinating
passage is that word, 'came', in verse 17. 'I came', says Jesus,
'to call the bad people, not the good ones.' Pause a moment
before we even think about the bad and the good. What does
Jesus mean, 'I came'? He implies that, like the builder and
his colleagues, he had 'come' with a specific purpose. But . . .
'come' from where? Isn't it an odd way of talking about a sense
of vocation? Might we not expect someone engaged in a
particular mission to speak of 'I've been called to . . .', rather
than 'I've come'?

I think this saying hints at something we noticed right at
the start of Mark's gospel: that Jesus was, simultaneously,
called to act out the part of Israel's Messiah, and to act out the
role of Israel's God, coming (yes!) to rescue his people at last,
to reveal his glory and establish his kingdom. I think this is
what we see here, reflected off the text in a sudden flicker of
light. There are echoes here, after all, of what God says in the
prophecy of Ezekiel, chapter 34. There, speaking of Israel as a
flock of sheep, God declares that he himself is going to come
and search for the lost and the strayed.

Jesus uses that image, too, of course, in various places, but here he chooses another one: that of the doctor. Imagine a doctor who was so keen to put on a good show that he filled up the hospital with healthy people! Not a lot of point in that. But the people who were keeping an eye out for Jesus and what he was doing – the 'legal experts' from the party of the 'Pharisees', a kind of self-appointed group of moral watchdogs – make out that they're shocked at Jesus keeping company with all the wrong people.

That, too, is significant. Why would anybody have worried about who Jesus was associating with? People can be friends, we assume, with anybody they like. Yes: but only if they're private citizens. You or I can be friends with the strange characters we happen to meet. But if the Prime Minister, or his wife, befriends some dodgy or shady person it reflects badly. It calls their judgment into question.

And Jesus wasn't acting as just another person on the street. He was already recognized as someone claiming to speak for God, claiming to announce that God was now becoming king in the new way he'd always promised. So he naturally became a target. Imagine the journalists and photographers swarming around someone who suddenly announces the foundation of a new political party! Everyone wants to know what signals are being sent, what lifestyle this person will adopt, and so on. That's what it was like with Jesus.

Jesus leaves them in no doubt: his new kingdom-of-God movement will be all about celebrating a new sort of healing. He's already been healing people's bodies, and now he uses that medical imagery to explain what's happening on a larger scale as well. Tax-collectors were no more popular in the ancient world than they are today. In fact, they were often even less popular, because they would be working for some regime or other – either the Romans, the hated pagans who were the ultimate overlords, or one of the Herod family, local but not much better. (The reason there was a tax-booth just along the seashore from Capernaum is that you would cross over from Herod Antipas' territory into that of his brother, Philip.) In a small community, everyone would know everyone else, and once someone was regarded as a bad character, that would be it. Nobody would want to be friends – except other people who had been treated in the same way.

And Jesus was determined to treat them differently. This was not (just to be clear) because, so to speak, God likes bad characters and wants them to stay as bad characters. No: God loves bad characters and wants to rescue them! Sometimes people today speak as though Jesus simply tells people that they're all right the way they are. That would be like a doctor filling the hospital with sick people and leaving them still sick.

When Jesus says 'Follow me!' it is, of course, a wonderful affirmation of who we are, deep down inside. You are a human being, made to reflect God's image and glory into the world, and Jesus is calling you to do just that in whatever specific way God wants from you. That is part of the message of Lent: a new calling.

But this doesn't mean we can continue to live in the ways we've always lived. On the contrary. When Jesus calls someone, said Dietrich Bonhoeffer, he commands them to come and die. We shall see that soon enough. The death begins right here, as the 'sick people' discover that Jesus heals them so that they leave that old life behind. But, as with the gospel as a whole, the death happens so that new life can grow in its place. When you hear Jesus calling, 'Follow me!', you should expect both. From sickness to health. From death to life.

Today

Help me, gracious Lord, to hear you calling, to celebrate your love, and to accept your healing in every area of my life.

SATURDAY AFTER ASH WEDNESDAY

Mark 1.9–15

⁹This is how it happened. Around that time, Jesus came from Nazareth in Galilee, and was baptized by John in the river Jordan. ¹⁰That very moment, as he was getting out of the water, he saw the heavens open, and the spirit coming down like a dove onto him. ¹¹Then there came a voice, out of the heavens: 'You are my son! You are the one I love! You make me very glad.'

¹²All at once the spirit pushed him out into the desert. ¹³He was in the desert forty days, and the satan tested him there. He was with the wild beasts, and angels waited on him.

¹⁴After John's arrest, Jesus came into Galilee, announcing God's good news.

¹⁵'The time is fulfilled!' he said; 'God's kingdom is arriving! Turn back, and believe the good news!'

Part of the fun of learning to read is learning to listen for echoes. If you were browsing in a bookshop and saw a novel with the title *Pride, Prejudice and Passion,* you would recognize at once that the author was echoing Jane Austen's novel *Pride and Prejudice.* If you were a Scottish football supporter and saw a headline saying 'Old Firm up to New Tricks', you would know at once that this referred to some new controversy involving the 'Old Firm', the two great Glasgow clubs, Rangers and Celtic. And if you switched on the television and heard the announcer describing a new series in which people were determined 'to boldly go' somewhere exotic or dangerous, you would recognize the echo of *Star Trek*. This echo recognition functions at every level of writing and speaking. The evidence suggests that it has always done so, ever since humans spoke and wrote words.

Part of the excitement of learning to read the Bible is listening for the echoes that one text sets up when it refers back to another – which the author assumes, or hopes, that you will already know. This passage is one of the classic examples. Jesus is baptized by John in the river Jordan, and as the spirit comes down on him like a dove there is a voice from heaven: 'You are my son! You are the one I love! You make me very glad.'

Now if this is the voice of God himself (and Mark clearly intends us to understand that that's what it is), then presumably God can say what he likes. But, as regularly in the New Testament, the 'new' thing God is doing and saying is the fulfilment, the coming-of-age if you like, of all kinds of things he had been saying in the Old Testament. And here there are two passages which those with sharp ears will be able to detect. Only if we pick up these echoes will we be able to 'hear' what Mark was wanting us to hear.

First, there is Psalm 2. It's a short, powerful poem about the kingdoms of the world and the kingdom of God. The world's kingdoms huff and puff and make a lot of noise, telling one another that they can do without God; and God looks down and laughs at them, installing his own appointed king, and warning the nations that they must submit to him. It's a vivid statement of the ancient Jewish hope, told and retold in one story after another.

And at its heart is the word of God to the king whom he is appointing to rule the nations. The king himself, in the poem, tells what he heard: 'I will tell of the decree of YHWH: He said to me, "You are my son; today I have begotten you. Ask of me, and I will make the nations your heritage, and the ends of the earth your possession."'

So Mark wants us to hear that the voice of God at Jesus' baptism is appointing him, as his own 'son', to the role of the king who will bring God's rule to bear on the foolish, warring nations. The second passage reinforces this and gives it particular direction. It's from the first of the 'servant' poems in Isaiah 40—55: 'Here is my servant, whom I uphold, my chosen, in whom my soul delights. I have put my spirit upon him; he will bring forth justice to the nations.'

The 'servant', then, is the one who makes God very glad, and who will be the means through which God's justice will extend into all the world. But, as we read on in Isaiah, we discover how the 'servant' is going to do this. It will happen through his own suffering and cruel, shameful death.

There is no doubt, as we read on through Mark's gospel, that these are the themes that the author wanted us to hear, as 'echoes', right up front. And, as we do so, we should see how they help him to get us on track for his larger theme of God's kingdom.

Jews of Jesus' day associated the idea of God becoming king with the ancient memory of their great story, the Exodus. That's when God brought them out of slavery, through the Red Sea, into the desert, and then through the river Jordan into the promised land. That's what it meant, in another ancient song, for God to become king (Exodus 15.18). Now Jesus is, as it were, leading the way through the water into the new world, the new time, the new possibility. He goes into the desert for forty days, like the Israelites in the desert for forty years. Then back he comes, and makes the announcement: 'This is the time! God is becoming king, right now!'

This is the 'good news' for which Israel had longed (another 'echo', this time of Isaiah 40.9 and 52.7). And anyone who hears this message must also hear another one, the one to which we pay special attention in Lent: 'Turn back' – turn back from doing things your own way, from organizing your life according to your own hopes and whims. If God is becoming king, and if Jesus is being installed as the human king through whom God's kingdom is now happening, the only appropriate reaction is to abandon our own little hopes and schemes and let God be God in our lives. And through our lives.

Today

Lord Jesus, Son of the living God, help us to believe that you are the world's true king, and to turn back from all that gets in the way of your rule in our lives.

WEEK 1: SUNDAY

Psalm 25.1–10

[1]To you, O LORD, I lift up my soul.
[2]O my God, in you I trust;
   do not let me be put to shame;
   do not let my enemies exult over me.
[3]Do not let those who wait for you be put to shame;
   let them be ashamed who are wantonly treacherous.

[4]Make me to know your ways, O LORD;
   teach me your paths.
[5]Lead me in your truth, and teach me,
   for you are the God of my salvation;
   for you I wait all day long.

[6]Be mindful of your mercy, O LORD, and of your steadfast love,
   for they have been from of old.
[7]Do not remember the sins of my youth or my transgressions;
   according to your steadfast love remember me,
   for your goodness' sake, O LORD!

[8]Good and upright is the LORD;
   therefore he instructs sinners in the way.
[9]He leads the humble in what is right,
   and teaches the humble his way.
[10]All the paths of the LORD are steadfast love and faithfulness,
   for those who keep his covenant and his decrees.

I met a friend the other day who is working on the great Victorian missionary and explorer David Livingstone (1813–73). Livingstone was a great hero to nineteenth-century Christians: he combined evangelistic zeal with a restless hunger for both geographical and scientific exploration, and – long before people became cynical about such things – he genuinely believed that he was bringing 'civilization' to the vast and hitherto unmapped interior of Africa. 'I am prepared to go anywhere,' he said, 'provided it be forward.' We today might want to point out the folly of blundering on into the unknown, and of doing things that might have, to say the least, more ambiguous results than he intended. But there is no doubting his sheer courage and energy, which puts most of us (whose efforts are no doubt equally ambiguous, though on a more domestic scale) to shame.

But I was put in mind of such visionary exploration when praying through this Psalm; because it is the prayer of someone who has heard God's call to set off and go somewhere but is, as yet, quite uncertain where that 'somewhere' is. This, to be sure, has been a common experience of God's people down the ages. There are several times, in the book of Acts, that great tale of early missionary expansion, when Paul and his companions are not sure where to go next, and have to wait in puzzlement for further instructions.

So the prayer at the heart of the Psalm is in verses 4 and 5: 'Make me to know your ways, O LORD; teach me your paths. Lead me in your truth, and teach me.' That should be our prayer day by day, and especially now as we've set off on this Lenten journey. (Experience of past Lents suggests that it can be a time when those who take it seriously find that, like the early explorers, they are going out into a country they don't know, full of unforeseen hazards as well as glorious possibilities.)

But the problem is not just that we don't know where we're going. There are two other difficulties which we will be all too aware of. First, there seem to be hostile forces all around us. The first Sunday of Lent, when traditionally we reflect on Jesus' temptations, is often a day for reflecting on our temptations as well. Anyone determining to make a fresh start, and to go forward with Jesus into the unknown, is almost bound to find that testing of one sort or another increases dramatically. I was talking recently to a friend who, after many years of pondering God's call, is finally going forward for training for full-time ministry. Almost at once things began to go wrong: serious sickness in the family, financial problems, sharp opposition from friends believing this was a mistake. This is classic. It's like what happens when you're out for a walk and suddenly come out from behind a high wall into the teeth of a gale. That's when you need to pray, with the Psalmist, 'Do not let my enemies exult over me!' (verse 2).

But as well as hostile forces (and perhaps hostile people) there are forces within which can be just as threatening. Here we find four: the sense of shame that will come if we blunder off in the wrong direction (verses 2, 3); our past mistakes and downright sins (verse 7); and, in the later part of the Psalm beyond the verses set for today, loneliness (verse 16) and other 'troubles of the heart' (verse 17). They are all familiar, especially to those who set off on the Lenten path of following the Lord without knowing where he's leading.

But, as so often in the Psalms, the answer is found in the character of God himself, the God we know and see in Jesus. He is trustworthy (verse 2); his ways are truth, and he provides salvation, rescue (verse 5); above all, he is merciful and constant in his love (verses 6, 7). He is good and upright (verse 8). There are times when we need to pick up these attributes of God, almost like picking up a set of large bricks or stones, and place them like stepping-stones, one after the other, in the river we are trying to cross. That is part of what it means to 'wait' on God (verse 5).

Then we can walk ahead, not because we know the way or are feeling especially brave, but because we know there is solid ground under our feet. This is not folly; it is humility (verse 9). And if we're waiting for the Lord and relying on him, we will naturally want (as, left to ourselves, we often do not naturally want) to keep his covenant and his decrees (verse 10). Obedience, in fact, arises most naturally not from an 'ethic' being forced on us against our will, but from that sense of humility which comes when we know we don't know the way but trust that God does. The first Sunday of Lent is the time for looking the enemies in the face and naming them before God. It is also the time to look God in the face and learn to trust him for every step of the way.

Today

Lead me, O Lord, in your truth, and teach me, for you are the God of my salvation.

WEEK 1: MONDAY

Mark 2.18–28: focused on 2.18–22

[18]John's disciples, and the Pharisees' disciples, were fasting. People came and said to Jesus, 'Look here: John's disciples are fasting, and so are the Pharisees' disciples; why aren't yours?'

[19]'How can the wedding guests fast', Jesus replied, 'if the bridegroom is there with them? As long as they've got the bridegroom with them, they can't fast.

[20]'Mind you, the time is coming when the bridegroom will be taken away from them. They'll fast then all right.

[21]'No one sews unshrunk cloth onto an old cloak. If they do, the new patch will tear the old cloth, and they'll end up with a worse hole. [22]Nor does anyone put new wine into old wineskins. If they do, the wine will burst the skins, and they'll lose the wine and the skins together. New wine needs new skins.'

I am writing this not long after the worldwide commemorations that took place on the tenth anniversary of the terrible terrorist attacks on New York and Washington on September 11, 2001. In many countries around the globe, people stopped what they were doing and paused to remember, and shudder. Many wept. There were church services, solemn music, the reading out of names.

Some great and terrible events are felt to be so important that only a pause, only a solemn commemoration, will do. It seems to be quite wrong that you should have a party or a dance, or indeed a wedding, at such a time. Can you imagine the effect if, as the commemorations in New York were at their height, a clown and a juggler had burst out of the crowd and started to perform funny, silly antics to make the crowds laugh?

People would have been shocked. The police would probably have come and hustled the troublemakers away.

Nobody knows how long America will go on commemorating that horrible day. But the Jewish people of Jesus' day had been commemorating other disasters, as great as those of September 11 and much greater, for centuries. They looked back to the terrible events when Babylon had come and destroyed Jerusalem, burnt the Temple to the ground, and taken the people into captivity in a land far away. Only the most solemn commemoration would do if the people were to recall, with due solemnity, events that traumatic. So, like New Yorkers on September 11, the Jewish people kept special days when they fasted and prayed and remembered. That was part of their national identity. It was part of what made them who they were. Everyone who wanted to take the great national story seriously would join in.

But Jesus' disciples were not joining in. They were not fasting when all the others were. And so, like people laughing and playing at a 9/11 commemoration, they scandalized those who saw them. 'Why aren't your disciples fasting?'

Jesus' reply explains, in a vivid and explosive little image, what is going on. This has nothing to do (as people sometimes imagine) with Judaism being 'legalistic' and Jesus being eager to abolish 'rules'. It has nothing to do with Jews trying to impress God with their moral effort and Jesus telling them that you don't have to do that after all. It has everything to do with what Jesus has already been saying: *the time is fulfilled, and God's kingdom is arriving!* Jesus wasn't teaching a new kind of 'religion', or a different 'moral code'. He was launching the project that was designed to fulfil all Israel's dreams, to undo the long years of shame and sorrow and replace them with a great celebration, a sort of wedding party.

Jesus, in other words, is explaining his disciples' failure to fast on the appropriate days by claiming that this moment, the time of his public career, is the long-awaited special time, the time when God and Israel are getting it together again at last. The picture of the wedding party looks back to various biblical passages, and highlights the extraordinary claim that Jesus himself is the 'bridegroom', who has come to celebrate his wedding. There is no way the wedding guests can fast while that's going on – though (in a typical dark aside, because God's kingdom will only come through his suffering and death) there will come a moment of fasting, of utter desolation, when 'the bridegroom is taken away'.

Jesus then broadens out the picture. You don't stick a new patch on an old coat, or put new wine into old wineskins. You can't, in other words, patch up the old life of Judaism with a little bit of kingdom-teaching. You can't expect to squash the new life of the kingdom into the old bottles of Judaism.

This is not, to repeat, because there was anything wrong with Judaism. The Jews were God's people, struggling to be faithful to God's covenant. No: the covenant itself was looking forward to the time when God would do the new thing he'd always promised. Now he was fulfilling that promise, even though it didn't look like what most people had expected. And when that moment arrives, you can't hold on to the old ways. Candles are great when it's dark, but when the sun rises you need to blow them out.

People have often quoted this passage about 'new wineskins' to justify innovations in the church. Fair enough, up to a point. God is still the God of surprises and new ideas. But the main point, far deeper than all our small rearrangements of the furniture, is that, with the coming of Jesus, Israel and the world were given not a new set of rules, not a new type of 'religion', but new creation itself.

So isn't it a bit odd, as we get into the stride of our Lenten disciplines, to talk about Jesus and his disciples refusing to fast? Not a bit of it. It's because of that new creation, launched once and for all with Jesus himself, that we need to take time and make the effort to bring our lives into line with the new reality. We do not fast because we commemorate some great national disaster. We fast because, as those already caught up in Jesus' kingdom-project, in God's new world, we need to be sure that we are saying a firm goodbye to everything in us that still clings to the old.

Today

Help us, gracious Lord, to be wise in our disciplines, to celebrate your new life and to put to death all that detracts from it.

WEEK 1: TUESDAY
Mark 3.1–19; focused on 3.13–19

[13]Jesus went up the mountain, and summoned the people he wanted, and they came to him. [14]He appointed twelve (naming them 'apostles') to be with him and to be sent out as heralds, [15]and to have authority to cast out demons. [16]In appointing the Twelve, he named Simon 'Peter'; [17]James, son of Zebedee, and his brother John, he named 'Boanerges', which means 'sons of thunder'. The others were [18]Andrew, Philip, Bartholomew, Matthew, Thomas, James son of Alphaeus, Thaddaeus, Simon the Cananaean, [19]and Judas Iscariot (the one who handed him over).

You know the revolution has become serious when its leaders appoint an alternative government. The Western world watched and waited in the early months of 2011 as the Libyan rebels set up a kind of shadow body. There was still a 'government' in Tripoli, loyal to the long-time leader, Colonel Gaddafi, but away to the north-east, in one of the rebel strongholds, the increasingly influential rebel movement set up a body to administer the larger and larger area under its control.

Until we realize that Jesus' calling of the Twelve must have felt a bit like that, we won't get to the heart of what was going on. He was, after all, behaving as if he was already in charge – speaking with authority, and backing up his words with decisive and startling actions. This had already aroused hostility and threats from the existing authorities, both real and self-appointed. Undeterred, Jesus moved ahead. His next action spoke volumes.

Anyone behaving as if they're in charge, and then calling people and giving them new names and an apparently special role, is quite obviously making a statement. He is, it seems, consolidating his position. He isn't just a maverick, going around doing bizarre and surprising things. He seems to have some kind of strategy.

But the strategy has a clear symbolic value. Numbers speak volumes. If Jesus had given his followers ten new 'commandments', the point would have been obvious: these were to replace the ten given by God through Moses on Mount Sinai. What Jesus does is equally obvious to anyone with the least knowledge of ancient Israel and of the Jewish hopes of the first century.

The people of Israel were a *family*, tracing ancestry back to the patriarchs Abraham, Isaac and Jacob. Jacob had had twelve sons, some of whom became famous (Reuben, Simeon, Levi, and above all Judah, Joseph and Benjamin) and some of whom remained less so (Naphtali, Issachar, Asher, Gad, Zebulun and Dan). The great primal collection of biblical books, the first five (from Genesis to Deuteronomy) places special emphasis on the Twelve and their particular callings.

When the Israelites finally entered the promised land after their forty-year wander in the desert, Joshua parcelled out the land between the twelve tribes, with the descendants of Levi living and working as priests and teachers among the others. After many generations, disaster struck: the northern tribes were carried away captive by the Assyrians. Nobody really knew where they were, or whether they had been simply dispersed. Only the tribes of Benjamin and Judah, and such Levites as lived among them, remained. Up till then, the people had been known as 'Israelites', the twelve sons of Jacob (whose special name, given by God, was 'Israel'). Now they would be known as the 'Judah-people'. That's where the modern word 'Jew' comes from.

But there were some great, ancient prophets who had predicted that when God restored the fortunes of his people he would call the twelve tribes back into existence. There can be no doubt that this is the message Jesus wanted to convey when he called twelve from among his followers, and spoke of them as such. This was not simply a renewal of 'Judaism', the Judah-people. This was a renewal of Israel itself. This was a going-back-to-the-beginning move. It was almost as powerful, and as dangerous, a ploy as it would be today if an apparently self-appointed leader were to call a press conference in front of Buckingham Palace or on the White House lawn, or were to build a new official house and call *it* 'Buckingham Palace' or 'The White House'.

Two other features of Jesus' call of the Twelve stand out particularly. First, it forces us to ask, as do Jesus' actions: who does he think he is? He is not the first of the Twelve, a kind of 'first among equals'. No: he calls the Twelve into existence. That makes him at least a new Jacob. But perhaps he is going further. It is, after all, God himself who called the people of Israel to be his people.

The second feature reinforces this first one. Jesus gives to some of the Twelve new names. He names Simon 'Peter', which means 'rock' or 'stone'. James and John, the two sons of Zebedee, he names 'Boanerges', which means 'thunder-sons'. But this is, more or less, what God had done with some of the original patriarchs. God renamed Abram 'Abraham', 'father of many nations' (Genesis 17.5). He renamed Jacob 'Israel', 'prince with God' (Genesis 32.28; 35.10). The new name carries a meaning, and the meaning indicates the purpose of God.

We might, perhaps, have been tempted to pass over this list of the Twelve. We don't know very much about most of them (a bit like the original twelve Israelite patriarchs, in fact). But the fact that there were twelve of them speaks more powerfully than any individual achievements. And it speaks right through the ages to us as well. The early Christians were quite clear that though Jesus had called the Twelve as a foundation for his work, he had then built on this foundation, and was continuing to do so (Ephesians 2.20). And Jesus himself promises, in the book of Revelation (2.17), that he will give a special 'new name' to all those who 'conquer', who hold out in the war against wickedness and corruption.

This promise holds firm and good for every single one of Jesus' followers today. Read the list of names slowly once more, only this time, in between each of the Twelve whom Jesus called, place the names of your Christian leaders, teachers and friends. Right in the middle, place your own name. And pray that God will enable you to hear him call you once more by name, as he called you in your baptism, and show you how you, too, can be part of his alternative government, his project of kingdom and renewal.

Today

Almighty God, you called Abraham, Isaac, Jacob and the Twelve; and, through Jesus, you called the twelve apostles. Call us afresh today; name us once more to carry forward your purposes in the world.

WEEK 1: WEDNESDAY
Mark 3.20–35; focused on 3.20–30

[20]He went into the house. A crowd gathered again, so that they couldn't even have a meal. [21]When his family heard it, they came to restrain him. 'He's out of his mind,' they said.

[22]Experts who had come from Jerusalem were saying, 'He is possessed by Beelzebul! He casts out demons by the prince of demons!'

[23]Jesus summoned them and spoke to them in pictures. 'How can the Accuser cast out the Accuser? [24]If a kingdom splits into two factions, it can't last; [25]if a household splits into

23

two factions, it can't last. [26]So if the Accuser revolts against himself and splits into two, he can't last – his time is up! [27]But remember: no one can get into a strong man's house and steal his property unless first they tie up the strong man; then they can plunder his house.

[28]'I'm telling you the truth: people will be forgiven all sins, and all blasphemies of whatever sort. [29]But people who blaspheme the holy spirit will never find forgiveness. They will be guilty of an eternal sin.' [30]That was his response to their claim that he had an unclean spirit.

I stood by the side of the stream and scratched my head. There used to be a bridge there, but it had been washed away in a storm some years before. I suspect the locals – this was in a remote area of the Scottish highlands – were quite happy that it hadn't been rebuilt. No cars, not even tractors, could drive any further up their unspoilt valley. Now only walkers could pass that way; and the only walkers who could do it would be those prepared to ford the stream.

There were only two solid rocks I could see that would give me a firm foothold. For the rest, I'd have to splash and hope; but I knew if I made it, first to one rock, then to the other, I'd get across all right. It worked.

For generations people reading the gospels have wondered, quite naturally, just how much they can trust the gospels. Sceptics have suggested that it was all made up later to boost the church's picture of the Jesus it worshipped. The bridges to historical certainty have been broken and not rebuilt. Fundamentalists have said that it was all dictated by God, so the question doesn't arise. But most ordinary Christians are somewhere in between. Where are there solid footholds on which we know we can stand, even if it feels a bit of a splash, sometimes, to get to them?

This passage is one of those solid rocks. Nobody in the early church, however inventive they were feeling, would ever have made up a story about Jesus being accused of being in league with the devil. That would simply give too much ammunition to the new movement's opponents, of whom there were plenty. So we can be absolutely sure this story is historically solid. You can rest your whole weight on it.

But if this story is solid, it means that we are forced, whether we want to or not, to believe that Jesus really was doing and saying things that were so remarkable that the only possible explanation – unless Jesus really was acting with a new, God-given power – was that he was in league with the devil. His opponents must have been desperate; this was all they could come up with. They couldn't deny that Jesus had been doing extraordinary things. They could only try to hit back with smear and innuendo. The solid rock at one point enables us, then, to walk through some other bits of the fast-moving historical stream with equal confidence.

So what do we find as we do so? We find a new level of a theme we already observed: that when Jesus was behaving as if he was in charge, it wasn't just the human 'authorities' that were being upstaged, and likely to strike back. It was the dark powers that hovered behind them.

There is an irony here. The legal experts from Jerusalem say that Jesus is in league with 'the Accuser', in other words, 'the satan'. The word 'satan' actually means 'accuser'; this reflects the ancient belief that the dark force in question was God's 'director of public prosecutions', whose job it was to point the finger at evildoers, and who enjoyed the role so much that he began to incite people to commit offences for which he could then charge them. But it is they, themselves, who are 'accusing' – accusing Jesus! This is part of a much larger theme which continues throughout Mark's gospel, as various different people 'accuse' Jesus of all sorts of things until they end up crucifying him.

But Jesus, in response, makes his strongest claim yet about what is going on through his work. What he is doing indicates clearly that the 'Accuser's' kingdom – the usurped rule, in the whole world, of the power of evil – is being broken. Jesus has already made a decisive impact on it, 'binding the strong man' so that he can now 'plunder his house' (verse 27). This is the only explanation, Jesus is suggesting, that fits the facts. If Jesus had been in league with the satan, things would have got worse, not better.

The sharp, and worrying, warnings of verses 28–30 have often been taken out of context, as though there was a special 'unforgiveable sin' but Jesus wasn't telling us what it was. Within the passage, though, the meaning is clear. Jesus is doing what he is doing by the power of the holy spirit. But if people look at the spirit's work and declare that it's the work of the devil, they are erecting a high steel wall between them and the powerful, rescuing love of God. That is a warning to all of us, whenever we are tempted to sneer at some new or different 'Christian' movement.

The main lesson for us, though, as we continue our journey through Lent, may well be this. If we are serious about following Jesus, people will misunderstand us, too, and may accuse us of bad motives, or prejudice, or 'extremism'. The answer is simply to look back to Jesus, and to his victory over all the powers of evil. They can still make a lot of noise, and cause a lot of nuisance, but the 'strong man' has been tied up, and those who work for God's kingdom can indeed, in the power of the spirit, set about plundering his house.

Today

Teach us, Lord Jesus, not to fear the accusations of the enemy, but to trust in your victory at all times.

WEEK 1: THURSDAY

Mark 4.1–20; focused on 4.1–9

¹Once again Jesus began to teach beside the sea. A huge crowd gathered; so he got into a boat and stationed himself on the sea,

with all the crowd on the shore looking out to sea. [2]He taught them lots of things in parables. This is how his teaching went.

[3]'Listen!' he said. 'Once upon a time there was a sower who went out sowing. [4]As he was sowing, some seed fell beside the path, and the birds came and ate it up. [5]Other seed fell on the rock, where it didn't have much soil. There was no depth to the ground, so it shot up at once; [6]but when the sun came up it was scorched, and withered away, because it hadn't got any root. [7]Other seed fell in among thorns; the thorns grew up and choked it, and it didn't give any crop. [8]And other seeds fell into good soil, and gave a harvest, which grew up and increased, and bore a yield, in some cases thirtyfold, in some sixtyfold, and in some a hundredfold.'

[9]And he added, 'If you've got ears, then listen!'

From where I am sitting I can see, out in the autumn fields, the farmer harvesting the corn. It isn't all in yet; some of the fields won't reach their full growth for another few weeks. But when I walk down the lane, or drive through mile after mile of golden grain gently waving in the wind, there is a strong sense of fulfilment. As far as the farms are concerned, this is the moment the whole year has been waiting for. This is what all the hard work has been about. It's time to draw it all together and celebrate the goodness of land, rain, sunshine and fresh air, all contributing to the great harvest.

It is not surprising, given that ancient Palestine had an almost entirely rural economy, that the theme of harvest was a powerful image in the ancient scriptures, pointing forwards to the time when God would fulfil his promises at last. What's more, when things had gone badly wrong – when God's people had gone away into exile in Babylon – some of the prophets spoke not just of a coming harvest, but of a fresh 'sowing'. God would 'sow' his people again in their land, so that the new harvest, when it came, would be the result of a fresh act, a renewal of the covenant.

This, I believe, is why Jesus chose to speak about, and Mark chose to highlight, this idea of the seed being sown – and much of it apparently going to waste. With this famous parable, Jesus is saying two things in particular. The crowds were eager for the first, but not for the second.

The people who crowded to the shore to hear him (the northern shore of the sea of Galilee, around Capernaum, has several natural amphitheatres where someone speaking from a boat can easily be heard by thousands) had, indeed, come in the hope of hearing the first point. As for the second, they may have found it not just unwelcome but incredible. Perhaps that is why Jesus had to say it in 'parables', teasing stories ending 'if you've got ears, then hear'. When you say that sort of thing, you expect people to hear you hint that 'I am saying something important but cryptic here, and you've got to decode it . . . perhaps because it's dangerous'.

The first thing, for which his hearers were on tiptoe with excitement, was the good news that the 'sowing' was indeed happening at last. Jesus' kingdom-movement was indeed the long-awaited restoration of God's people. The hints, signs and symbols that Jesus had been putting out were true. This was the moment! Everything was going to be different! God would liberate his people at last!

But the second, so surprising and unwelcome, was that God's great kingdom-action, bursting in upon them through Jesus' words and works, was not having the effect that one might have imagined. The seed was being sown, but a lot of it seemed to be doing no good at all. Birds were eating some of it. Other seed produced quick-growing plants without any root. Other seed was choked by thorns. Jesus is under no illusions, and he wants his hearers to be clear as well: yes, this is God's long-awaited new work, but no, it doesn't mean that God's people can simply be affirmed, or their national aspirations underwritten, as they stand. As the ancient prophets had always warned, when God finally does the new thing he's promised, it is bound to be a work of judgment as well as mercy. That is what Jesus' contemporaries (just like us) don't want to hear.

Jesus was warning his contemporaries that, just because they were Jews, just because they were, as it were, part of God's team – and, as well, just because they had suffered for their heritage – that didn't automatically mean that they would be the sort of soil that would produce a great harvest. They might well find that Jesus' kingdom-message was exciting, while they were listening to it, but not immediately relevant to this or that situation in their lives . . . Or they might think it was *so* exciting that they should rush off and do something right away, but without really thinking about it . . . Or they might try to combine following Jesus with all the usual concerns of everyday life . . .

One way or another, things would go wrong. Even though God's kingdom-project was indeed going ahead, many of those you might have expected to be front and centre in taking it forward would, like T. S. Eliot's Macavity the Mystery Cat, mysteriously be 'not there'.

Now this, I believe, was a very specific and urgent warning to Jesus' contemporaries. God's kingdom was going ahead – there really would be a bumper harvest, thirtyfold, sixtyfold and a hundredfold. But they might not be part of it, however much they thought it was theirs by right, and however much enthusiasm they felt for it at the moment. As so often, however, what was specific to Jesus' first hearers can then be 'translated' as the message we need to hear, and to speak, today. Anyone who knows the state of Christian faith and life in the wider world today can be in no doubt that, despite the decline in church attendances in the Western world, the seed is being sown in all kinds of ways. New, enthusiastic movements are springing up all over the place. This parable issues a warning, not least to the leaders of such movements: how deep are the roots going? What protection are you offering against the birds and the thorns? Today's excitement can easily become tomorrow's boredom, or worse. Some of the 'new atheists' were once – for a short while – keen Christians. Evangelists, church planters and pastors, take note.

Today

Grant us, sovereign Lord, to nurture the seed of the word, to guard it and let it grow, and to bring forth a harvest to your glory.

WEEK 1: FRIDAY

Mark 4.21–41; focused on 4.35–41

[35]That day, when it was evening, Jesus said to them, 'Let's go over to the other side.'

[36]They left the crowd, and took him with them in the boat he'd been in. There were other boats with him too.

[37]A big windstorm blew up. The waves beat on the boat, and it quickly began to fill. [38]Jesus, however, was asleep on a cushion in the stern. They woke him up.

'Teacher!' they said to him, 'We're going down! Don't you care?'

[39]He got up, scolded the wind, and said to the sea, 'Silence! Shut up!'

The wind died, and there was a flat calm. [40]Then he said to them, 'Why are you scared? Don't you believe yet?'

[41]Great fear stole over them. 'Who *is* this?' they said to each other. 'Even the wind and the sea do what he says!'

One of the things I love about the Psalms is the direct, in-your-face way the poet speaks to God. 'Wake up, God!' says the Psalmist; it's time to call the wicked to account (7.6). 'Wake up! I need someone to help me!' (35.23); 'Rouse yourself! Why are you asleep? Wake up, don't cast us away!' (44.23). 'Wake up and show the pagans who's boss!' (59.5). The prophet Isaiah says much the same (51.9): 'Wake up, wake up, Arm of the LORD – show us how strong you are!'

I suspect, of course, that if we'd sat these poets down in a cool, easy moment and asked them, 'Did you really think God was asleep?', they might have said, 'Well, no; he is God, after all; but it certainly *seemed* as though he'd gone to sleep at the time!' That, it seems, is a fairly typical expression of what we might call biblical faith: faith in a God whom we believe at one level to be all-seeing, never-sleeping, omnipresent and omnicompetent – but who, at another level, seems, from the perspective of our muddled and messy lives, to have gone to sleep on the job.

That's why I find this passage in Mark so wonderfully encouraging. Right from the start the early Christians, reading this short but remarkable account, found it to be a great source of strength and comfort. The little ship of the church is tossed to and fro by the wind and on the waves. There are many, many times when both church leaders and rank-and-file Christians really do feel as though all is lost. All they can do at such times is to pray in the way the first disciples did on the boat.

Whether or not they realized, at the time, how exactly they were echoing the Psalms, Mark certainly did. He realized, too, the way in which the whole story carried all sorts of other echoes as well. Again, the Psalms: when people cry to YHWH, Israel's God, from the midst of the storm, he will make it to be still and quieten the waves (65.7; 89.9; 107.29). In particular, God made the Red Sea to part for his people to walk through; that is central, of course, to the great story of the Exodus. Now here is Jesus, doing much the same thing only close up and personal.

The disciples ask the natural question: 'Who *is* this?' Mark wants his readers to supply the answer, not in a glib or easy way, but with the same awe and breathless wonder of the frightened little group on the boat. 'Great fear stole over them,' he says. You bet it did. And unless it steals over us, too, as we roll around in our minds the possibility that when we're looking at Jesus we're looking at Israel's God in person, we are using the truth of the Incarnation as an intellectual screen behind which to hide for safety, rather than as the lens through which the light and warmth of God can flood and transform our hearts and lives.

Mark places this story at the end of his long chapter on parables. And, though he clearly wants us to see this as something which actually, and dramatically, happened, it too is a sort of parable. The parables left people with questions that they had to answer for themselves. This story left the disciples with questions that would take them a while to figure out properly. Mark, arranging his gospel like this, is saying to us (among other things) that part of the way the kingdom of God works is precisely by people having sudden and alarming questions raised in their minds which they will have to ponder and puzzle over.

Sometimes these questions are forced on us by events that are frightening and worrying at the time. Sometimes they grow slowly out of things we have read in the Bible or heard in church. This is normal and natural, however unsettling it may seem at the time. 'Don't you believe yet?' asks Jesus, almost teasing his frightened followers. This theme continues: 'Don't you get it? Don't you understand? You still don't get it?' (8.17, 21). Part of the point of Christian discipleship is to have our minds and imaginations challenged, opened, stretched, reshaped. The world – God's world! – is quite different, and a lot more unpredictable and interesting, than we often suppose. And at the heart of it is Jesus himself, sometimes apparently asleep but ready to wake up, transform our scary situations, and bounce the question back to us. When we pray 'Wake up, Lord!' we need to be prepared for him to reply that it is we who have been asleep. Our wake-up call to God is often the moment when God's wake-up call to us is finally getting through.

Today

Wake us up, O Lord, from our easy-going sleep. Help us always to remember that you are in control, no matter how frightening or alarming things may be.

WEEK 1: SATURDAY

Mark 8.31–38

[31]Jesus now began to teach them something new.

'There's big trouble in store for the son of man,' he said. 'The elders, the chief priests and the scribes are going to reject

him. He will be killed – and after three days he'll be raised.'
[32]He said all this quite explicitly.

At this, Peter took him aside and started to scold him. [33]But he turned round, saw the disciples, and scolded Peter.

'Get behind me, Accuser!' he said. 'You're thinking human thoughts, not God's thoughts.'

[34]He called the crowd to him, with his disciples. 'If any of you want to come the way I'm going,' he said, 'you must say "no" to your own selves, pick up your cross, and follow me. [35]Yes: if you want to save your life, you'll lose it; but if you lose your life because of me and the Message you'll save it. [36]After all, what use is it to win the world and lose your life? [37]What can you give in exchange for your life? [38]If you're ashamed of me and my words in this cheating and sinning generation, the son of man will be ashamed of you when he "comes in the glory of his father with the holy angels".'

Fans of detective stories will know the drill. The main lines of the plot are reasonably clear, or so it appears. But somewhere on the way there will be a clue, a hint, a nudge, which the alert reader will pick up. The culprit will have left a trace; something said that doesn't quite ring true, something done which seems a little out of character. The story may well be so gripping that the moment passes and the reader doesn't notice, or quickly forgets. But when the end comes, and all is revealed, that little incident, that small hint, will come into its own. 'Yes,' you will say, 'I should have known all along. That was the clue.'

At one level, this story in Mark is quite plain. Jesus is telling his disciples that he must go to Jerusalem and be killed – and that anyone who wants to follow him must be prepared for the same fate. We might well suppose, granted the violent history of Jewish uprisings in the folk memory of his hearers, that this sort of thing would hardly come as a surprise. But there is something more going on here than a clear-eyed recognition of the likely results of being involved in a 'kingdom-of-God' movement. Where is the hint?

The hint comes, I suggest, in Jesus' rebuke to Peter. Peter has started to scold Jesus: he would, perhaps, have been quite prepared (in theory at least) to risk his life to support Jesus, but it surely can't be right for Jesus himself to die! Jesus is the one they need to be king, not to throw his life away. Without Jesus, the whole movement is nothing.

Jesus could have said, by way of response, something like he says to the two disciples on the road to Emmaus (Luke 24). He could have launched into a lengthy Bible study, as he did then, to show that the whole theme and pattern of the scriptures was for God's people to be plunged into terrible trouble and misery and for God to do his new, rescuing work through that means. That's how it had always been, and if he was introducing the last in the line of God's great actions you might expect that it would have the same shape and pattern.

He could have done that; but he doesn't. Instead, he uses the sharpest possible language to scold Peter. 'Get behind me, Accuser!' he said. In other words, Peter has put into words not only the counsel of prudence, of common sense. Peter has blurted out what the Accuser, the satan, has been whispering to Jesus all along. 'You can't go and *die*; that will ruin it all! You're doing fine; some more healings, some more parables, people will get the message. Don't be silly; don't be rash; don't be melodramatic; slow and steady and it'll work out.' Sounds good, doesn't it? Almost a sigh of relief.

And Jesus recognizes the voice for what it is, even though it's coming through the lips of his own closest associate. It is the voice of the Accuser, the one who is always on the attack, always eager to undermine the work of God, always ready to lead people into more sin and more guilt so there will be more for him to accuse them of. *And Jesus is going to his death to take the weight of that accusation on to himself*, so that his people need bear it no longer.

At one level, of course, the Accuser is right. If Jesus goes and dies, that will ruin it all – it will ruin the enemy's plan to destroy God's people, God's plan, God's whole wonderful creation. Steer Jesus gently away from the cross, and he will die in his bed, of old age, leaving behind lots of good memories, lots of fine sayings, lots of healed cripples. And a world unredeemed. The cross is the means by which Jesus will rescue, not merely reform. It is the weapon with which he will not simply threaten the forces of evil, but overcome them. Peter's common-sense reaction (whoever heard of a crucified Messiah?) coincides exactly with the satanic opposition to God's saving plan. He is thinking human thoughts, not God's thoughts. By the time we get to Mark 15, we will understand why this hint is what it is and where it is. The little exchange between Peter and Jesus tells us, if we are alert, not just what will happen at the end of the story but what it all means.

Then comes the challenge from which most of us, given half a chance, still shrink. There is a sense in the gospel in which, because Jesus dies, we do not. His unique death saves us from what would otherwise be ours. But there is another sense, repeated again and again in the rest of the New Testament, that because Jesus dies, we must die too. We must pick up our cross – bearing public shame, as Jesus indicates in verse 38, as well as the prospect of pain and suffering – and follow him. That is not only the route by which we must travel for our own sakes. It is the path we tread through which Jesus' victory is made real, again and again, in the world. Common sense shrieks that this is crazy. Why not settle for a quiet life? But Jesus is quite clear. There are times when common sense means sliding along the smooth downward path with 'this cheating and sinning generation'. Don't rock the boat. Don't be an 'extremist'. Don't do anything rash. And behind this obvious, worldly advice there is the hidden message: don't talk about the cross. Don't mention Jesus. You don't want people to think you're a fanatic . . .

Well, there is of course always the danger of fanaticism, of a self-induced and self-promoting 'zeal'. But there is also the danger, and much modern Western Christianity runs this risk all the time, of being ashamed of the sharp-edged and scandalous message of the kingdom and the cross. I suspect many of us today need to be warned against the second more than the first.

Today

Forgive us, gracious Lord, when we have preferred human common sense to the strange wisdom and power of your cross. Give us strength and clarity of understanding to hear your call afresh and to follow wherever you lead.

WEEK 2: SUNDAY

Psalm 22.22–31

²²I will tell of your name to my brothers and sisters;
   in the midst of the congregation I will praise you:
²³You who fear the LORD, praise him!
   All you offspring of Jacob, glorify him;
   stand in awe of him, all you offspring of Israel!
²⁴For he did not despise or abhor
   the affliction of the afflicted;
   he did not hide his face from me,
      but heard when I cried to him.

²⁵From you comes my praise in the great congregation;
   my vows I will pay before those who fear him.
²⁶The poor shall eat and be satisfied;
   those who seek him shall praise the LORD.
   May your hearts live for ever!

²⁷All the ends of the earth shall remember
   and turn to the LORD;
and all the families of the nations
   shall worship before him.
²⁸For dominion belongs to the LORD,
   and he rules over the nations.

^{29}To him, indeed, shall all who sleep in the earth bow down;
   before him shall bow all who go down to the dust,
   and I shall live for him.
^{30}Posterity will serve him;
   future generations will be told about the Lord,
^{31}and proclaim his deliverance to a people yet unborn,
   saying that he has done it.

Imagine you are standing there in the dark, at the foot of the cross. The sun's light has failed, and through your tears all you can see is this horrible pole stretching up, with Jesus hanging there, his whole body so tortured that you can't even imagine the level of pain he must be in. You are cold, and afraid, and you hardly know what to do except stay there.

Gradually, slowly, as your eyes get used to the darkness, you find you can see a bit more clearly the upper parts of the cross. You can make out Jesus' arms, yanked almost out of their sockets, but stretching out in both directions. And then, above his head – though you can hardly bear to look, to see that face so battered and distorted – you can see the top of the central pole, with its sarcastic notice ('King of the Jews' – whoever heard of a crucified king!), nevertheless pointing upwards. And you find, coming from somewhere underneath all the sorrow and the sense of utter hopelessness, something else starting to make itself felt. Something about those two outstretched arms, that upward pointing sign. Something that resonates with the Psalm whose first verse Jesus had screamed out in his agony a few minutes ago (Mark 15.34). Something that might just begin to make sense, though a terrible and world-shaking sense, out of it all.

The Psalm verse Jesus had yelled out was of course the opening of Psalm 22: 'My God, my God, why have you forsaken me?' On and on goes the Psalm, plunging down to the depths of despair, of self-loathing, of helpless suffering. It is a place where many in our world still have to live. It is the place to which Jesus went on that black Friday afternoon. Sometimes it's all we can do to look at this suffering, going on and on like the cross itself, disappearing into the darkness.

But sometimes, as our eyes adjust, we can just glimpse something beyond, something that doesn't cancel out the suffering but that seems to grow out of it. Something that corresponds to the final verses of the Psalm, the verses we read today. These verses reach out, like the two arms on the cross; and they reach up, like the sign of the kingdom, pointing to the heavens. You can't split them off from the long, dark pole of the cross. Verses 22–31 depend entirely on the twenty-one verses that precede them. They are the fruit of the suffering. We read them today, a mere ten days into Lent, as an act, not of respite, as though they cancelled out the earlier part of the Psalm, but of encouragement. This is where it's all going, even if where we currently stand seems dark, dangerous and sad.

The first outstretched arm speaks of *rescue*, God's delivering of his people from all that has oppressed them. God hasn't abandoned the sufferer (verse 24). Those who are most in need will be given what they require (verse 26). As we stand there in the dark, let's learn to see that arm outstretched to the world that still needs it so badly.

The second outstretched arm speaks of *kingdom*. Astonishingly, God's kingdom is established over the whole world, over all the nations. This is deeply embedded in Israel's self-understanding. Such a notion is, of course, politically incorrect. There is no room for relativism in the Psalms. Either God is God of all the world or he's not God at all. 'All the ends of the earth shall remember and turn to the Lord': yes indeed, that is what it's all about. Only in him are to be found the justice and joy for which the world longs.

But, as we start to see these outstretched arms, we also see, high above the wounded face of Jesus, the cross pointing on upwards in what we now discern as an act of praise. 'I will tell of your name to my brothers and sisters' (verse 22); 'from you comes my praise in the great congregation' (verse 25);

'future generations' shall 'proclaim his deliverance to a people yet unborn' (verses 30 and 31). Pilate's mocking message, announcing Jesus as 'King of the Jews', comes true, not in the way he intended or expected but as something far stranger, far more world-shaking. Even when we can see nothing but darkness, the cross still points upwards to the God who makes even human wrath turn to his praise.

This cruel cross, planted roughly in the stony soil of Calvary, will thus bear fruit, fruit that will last: rescue, mission, praise. And we who find ourselves, this Lent, standing at its foot, in darkness and perhaps even despair, must learn to train our ears to hear these verses, not cut off from the rest of the Psalm but precisely growing out of it; must train our eyes to glimpse not just the broken body on the cross but the work of love, justice and worship that will result. Live with this Psalm as you stand by the cross. Watch and pray for the day when these final verses will become as real and obvious in our world as the darkness and suffering is right now.

Today

Help us, gracious Lord, so to stand in faith at the foot of the cross that the light can break through the darkness and guide us on our way.

WEEK 2: MONDAY

Mark 5.1–20

[1]So they came over the sea to the land of the Gerasenes. [2]When they got out of the boat, they were suddenly confronted by a man with an unclean spirit. [3]He was emerging from a grave-yard, which was where he lived. Nobody had been able to tie him up, not even with a chain; [4]he had often been bound with shackles and chains, but he used to tear up the chains and snap the shackles. No one had the strength to tame him. [5]On

and on, night and day, he used to shout out in the graveyard and on the hillside, and slash himself with stones.

[6]When he saw Jesus a long way away, he ran and threw himself down in front of him.

[7]'Why you and me, Jesus?' he shouted at the top of his voice. 'Why you and me, son of the High God? By God, stop torturing me!' – [8]this last, because Jesus was saying to him, 'Unclean spirit, come out of him!'

[9]'What's your name?' Jesus asked him.

'Legion,' he replied. 'That's my name – there are lots of us!' [10]And he implored Jesus not to send them out of the country.

[11]It so happened that right there, near the hillside, was a sizeable herd of pigs. They were grazing.

[12]'Send us to the pigs,' begged the spirits, 'so that we can enter them'.

[13]So Jesus gave them permission. The unclean spirits came out and went into the pigs. The herd rushed down the steep slope into the sea – about two thousand of them! – and were drowned.

[14]The herdsmen fled. They told it in the town, they told it in the countryside, and people came to see what had happened. [15]They came to Jesus; and there they saw the man who had been demon-possessed; who had had the 'legion', seated, clothed and stone-cold sober. They were afraid. [16]The people who had seen it all told them what had happened to the man – and to the pigs. [17]And they began to beg Jesus to leave their district.

[18]Jesus was getting back into the boat, when the man asked if he could go with him. [19]Jesus wouldn't let him.

'Go back home,' he said. 'Go to your people and tell them what the Lord has done for you. Tell them how he had pity on you.'

[20]He went off, and began to announce in the Ten Towns what Jesus had done for him. Everyone was astonished.

When Bertrand Russell wrote his famous book, *Why I am Not a Christian*, he listed various things about the life of Jesus which, he said, put him off. One was the story of Jesus cursing the fig tree (Mark 11.12–14, 20–24). Another was this incident: Russell objected to Jesus' apparently cavalier treatment of two thousand pigs. I have sometimes had atheists write to me, or speak to me after lectures, and repeat these same charges. Was Jesus not guilty of rough, violent treatment of the world of animals and plants?

Objections like these completely miss the point, and raise worrying questions about how serious Russell actually was in his consideration of Christianity. The gospels are not written to be a compendium of useful moral teaching and behaviour, to be offered to a world that simply needs good advice and good example. They are written to describe a one-off, unique moment in the history of the world. They make the sense they do only on the assumption that the world as a whole, and human beings in particular, and some human beings especially, are in an almighty mess and need a drastic rescue operation. They tell the story of how that dramatic and dangerous rescue operation was carried out.

In particular, they demand to be read at several different levels. (This is why I think Russell was hardly being serious. He must have known that most important books operate this way; one would hardly read a Shakespeare play simply as an interesting story of some Danish royalty, some Scottish noblemen, or some Italian families. True, Mark isn't Shakespeare; but he isn't a flat-footed one-dimensional writer, either.) There are several stories in the gospel that carry echoes and resonances far beyond their surface meaning, and this is one of them.

Whether or not (as some people think) Mark was written for the young church in Rome, everyone in the first-century Mediterranean world would know what a 'legion' was. It was the basic unit of the Roman army. Each legion comprised between five and six thousand men. There were Roman outposts across the Middle East, with the nearest legion itself based just to the north of Palestine, in Syria. Legions meant Roman power; and Roman power meant a smouldering resentment on the part of local people, who resented being ruled by foreigners, resented (and sometimes, dangerously, resisted) paying tax to them, and resented above all the insult to their national way of life because their own leaders (including the chief priests!) colluded with this pagan power. 'Legion' meant all of that and more.

With resentment there can come obsession. Suppose a Roman soldier had, with casual brutality, killed your best friend. Suppose a legionary had raped your daughter. You would go home that night fuming, furious but helpless. You would get up in the morning with this word hammering away in your head. Legion! Legion! Legion!

And with obsession there can come possession. Oh, I'm not pretending we can understand how that 'works'. There is nothing logical or easily analysed about destructive evil. It wouldn't be so dangerous if we could understand it. But I know that in this way, and in many others, ordinary people can, as it were, be taken over by strange forces. Sometimes they speak in their own voice. Sometimes, though, another voice – or several other voices – seem to be coming out of them. And the destructive nature of this 'possession' can often be seen in self-destructive behaviour. People who have worked in this area (I haven't done so very much, but I know and trust some who have) will recognize all this as depressingly familiar.

The story, then, seems to operate on at least three levels. First, there is the striking story of a very sick man being wonderfully healed and restored by Jesus. That, as always, is moving and powerful.

But second, underneath that, there is the shadow of a story that a great many first-century Jews longed to tell: the story of the Romans, with their legions, their garrisons, their sneering officials, their tax-collectors, and all their no-good works, being driven out of the country, out of the region, preferably down the hill into the Mediterranean Sea, never to return . . .

Third, linked to that, there is something going on here about Jesus' work on the edge of the Holy Land. The region he went into, that of the 'Gerasenes', is on the east side of the Sea of Galilee – disputed territory, then as now. And there was a herd of pigs, as there certainly wouldn't have been if the inhabitants had been living as good, law-abiding Jews, who of course didn't eat pork. There is an implicit challenge here: the story is an acted parable not only of cleansing the land of pagan pollution in the form of the Romans and their legions, but also, perhaps, of cleansing the land from the internal pollution of those who were sitting light to the ancestral codes (though this then stands in some tension with Mark 7, as we shall see).

Underneath it all is the larger picture, that of a God who never abandons anyone, no matter how 'far gone' they seem to be; of a Jesus who is acting with authority over all the 'forces' that rear their ugly heads in this world; of the spiritual power that can transform the saddest and most frightening of human situations (consider what it was like for the man's family, knowing the behaviour described in verse 4, and then being confronted with their brother, their son, perhaps their husband, their father, coming home cured). This, Mark is saying, is what it's like when God takes charge. It will be a bumpy ride, because the terrain is so uneven. But the kingdom is on the way.

Today

Grant us, good Lord, to reach out for your help no matter how appalling things may seem. Give us your healing and hope at every level of our lives.

WEEK 2: TUESDAY

Mark 5.21–43; focused on 5.25–34

[25]A woman who had had internal bleeding for twelve years heard about Jesus. [26](She'd had a rough time at the hands of one doctor after another; she'd spent all she had on treatment, and had got worse rather than better.) [27]She came up in the crowd behind him and touched his clothes. [28]'If I can just touch his clothes,' she said to herself, 'I'll be rescued.' [29]At once her flow of blood dried up. She knew, in her body, that her illness was cured.

³⁰Jesus knew at once, inside himself, that power had gone out of him. He turned around in the crowd and said, 'Who touched my clothes?'

³¹'You see this crowd crushing you,' said the disciples, 'and you say "Who touched me?"?'

³²He looked round to see who had done it. ³³The woman came up; she was afraid and trembling, but she knew what had happened to her. She fell down in front of him and told him the whole truth.

³⁴'My daughter,' Jesus said to her, 'your faith has rescued you. Go in peace. Be healed from your illness.'

I watched the bird take off from the field and, rising quickly into the sky, float and soar on the afternoon breeze. It was free, and expressing that freedom with a kind of light-hearted joy. I wondered, reading this story at the same time, what it would look like if that bird had been tied up, close to the ground, so that every time it wanted to fly free it found it was unable to do so. Even with the brain of a bird, such a poor creature would, we will suppose, be frustrated to the point of despair.

Now consider this woman who had suffered for twelve years from internal bleeding. She will, almost certainly, have been a family person; almost all women in that world were married, and most were mothers. But she won't have been free to be the wife and mother she would naturally have wanted. The bleeding will have been exhausting in itself, debilitating, sapping her energy all the time. But, far worse than that, she will have been constrained and constricted by a thousand necessary restrictions. These were not just insensitive or demeaning taboos. Good medical policy, granted what was known about at the time, would demand that such a person avoid the risk of infecting others. She was, technically speaking, 'unclean'. She was like a bird tethered to the ground. She could see everyone else free to live as they wished, but she was anchored, held back, by her seemingly incurable disease.

And yet . . . she made one final bid for the freedom that others had and she didn't. At considerable risk (because if people knew her condition they wouldn't have wanted her pushing past them through the crowd) she came up and touched Jesus. Making him, too, 'unclean' – according to the normal expectations.

But then the extraordinary thing happened. Instead of uncleanness flowing from her to him, a strange power seemed to flow out of him to her. (That in itself is remarkable. The gospels don't elsewhere speak of Jesus being aware of, as it were, a reservoir of power, which he could feel being drawn on when things like this happened.) Instead of him becoming unclean, she was cured. And the story all came tumbling out.

Jesus' response is very telling. 'My daughter,' he said, 'your faith has rescued you.' Your *faith*! Well, yes, it took a lot of faith to push through the crowd and come and touch him. If it didn't work, and if people discovered who she was, she would not be popular, to say the least. She had to believe that Jesus really could do what she longed for.

But wouldn't it have been more accurate, and perhaps theologically helpful, to say that it was God's power that had rescued her? Perhaps, in one sense. But we are here confronted with the truth that meets us all through the New Testament. Yes, of course God remains sovereign. Yes, of course it's Jesus who is in charge. But the God of the Bible chose from the beginning to act, wherever appropriate, *through* human beings. Humans were never meant to be mere spectators of God's work, or mere passengers, being carried along into God's future with their feet up. Humans were meant to participate, to worship God and so to be energized to live for him. And that begins with faith. There are many healing stories in which the person concerned seems not to be required to believe in advance. (The larger story which frames the present one, that of Jairus's daughter, is one such; the little girl was dead.) But there are many where Jesus himself puts the weight on faith.

All the power is from God, but the channel by which that is drawn down, perhaps on to the person of faith, perhaps on to the one for whom they are concerned, is human faith.

Stand with me at the edge of the crowd, and play the scene over again in your mind. Go slowly enough to recognize the range of emotions that pass through. Perhaps you know this woman and her condition; what do you feel and think as you see her shoving her way through the crowd? Have you ever felt like that before? And how do you feel, and what do you think, when you see Jesus stop and look round? Are you cross that he's been distracted from what he was on his way to do? (If you were Jairus, with your daughter on the point of death, you might well be frustrated at this interruption.) And what do you think about Jesus saying it was the woman's faith that had rescued her? Have you got faith like that? If not, are you just a little bit jealous?

Whatever your thoughts and feelings, seize the moment. Come up, yourself, in the crowd. Come close enough to Jesus so that you can talk together as he walks on towards Jairus's house. He will have enough time to listen to you, too. Perhaps he will ask you what you most want him to do for you. Perhaps he will challenge you: have you got faith? Do you want to be free, free as a bird?

Today

Give us, gracious Lord, the faith to come right up to you, to touch you in the crowd, to say what it is we need and want you to do for us.

WEEK 2: WEDNESDAY
Mark 6.1–29; focused on 6.14–29

[14]Jesus' name became well known, and reached the ears of King Herod.

'It's John the Baptist,' he said, 'risen from the dead! That's why these powers are at work in him.'

[15]Other people said, 'It's Elijah!'

Others said, 'He's a prophet, like one of the old prophets.'

[16]'No,' said Herod when he heard this. 'It's John. I cut off his head, and he's been raised.'

[17]What had happened was this. Herod had married Herodias, his brother Philip's wife. [18]John regularly told Herod it wasn't right for him to take his brother's wife; so Herod gave the word, arrested him and tied him up in prison. [19]Herodias kept up a grudge against him and wanted to kill him, but couldn't; [20]Herod was afraid of John, knowing that he was a just and holy man. So he protected him, and used to listen to him regularly. What he heard disturbed him greatly, and yet he enjoyed listening to him.

[21]And then, one day, the moment came. There was a great party. It was Herod's birthday, and he gave a feast for his leading retainers, militia officers, and the great and good of Galilee. [22]Herodias's daughter came in and danced, and Herod and his guests were delighted.

'Tell me what you'd like', said the king to the girl, 'and I'll give it you!'

[23]He swore to her, over and over again, 'Whatever you ask me, I'll give it you – right up to half my kingdom!'

[24]She went out, and said to her mother, 'What shall I ask for?'

'The head of John the Baptist,' she replied.

[25]So she went back at once to the king, all eager, and made her request: 'I want you to give me, right now, on a dish – the head of John the Baptist!'

[26]The king was distraught. But his oaths on the one hand, and his guests on the other, meant he hadn't the guts to refuse her. [27]So he sent a gaoler straight away with orders to bring John's head. He went and beheaded him in the prison, [28]brought the head on a dish, and gave it to the girl. The girl gave it to her mother.

[29]When John's followers heard about it, they came and took his body, and buried it in a tomb.

People sometimes have the idea that the world of the Bible is rather like the world of some old churches: quiet, serious, a bit old-fashioned, with nobody ever doing or saying anything to shock or frighten people. Sometimes, indeed, those who organize the biblical passages that are to be read out in churches seem deliberately to miss out the bits that might show how wrong that view is.

Certainly it's a good job we haven't missed out this passage, partly because it is indeed everything that people sometimes think the Bible is not and partly because it is quite important for the overall story Mark is telling us.

To begin with, of course, the behaviour of Herod and his family reads, even at two thousand years' distance, like the sort of thing you'd find in the gossip pages of a trashy magazine. A newspaper reporter once told a friend of mine that the stories that sell best include sex, royalty and religion; and this one has them all. In spades.

To begin with, we have the puppet monarch Herod Antipas. He was not a patch on his father, Herod the Great (the Herod who, in Matthew 2, had the babies in Bethlehem all killed). Like many second-generation pseudo-royalty, Antipas had discovered that he could basically organize his little world however he wanted . . . and so he did.

Trouble was, what he really wanted were two things: one, to be recognized as the true 'king of the Jews'; two, to have his brother's wife, Herodias. He got the second: he obtained a quickie divorce from his first wife, a foreign princess, and presumably there was some trouble with his brother, but it was that kind of family anyway. But, once that was fixed, there was no way he could ever be recognized by any but the most cynical Jews as their long-awaited rightful king.

This is where John the Baptist came in. He had been announcing that God's true king was on the way. And he made it only too clear that whoever this king might be it could not be old what's-his-name up the road, because God's anointed would never behave like that. So John was in trouble. Royalty, sex and religion: explosive.

But, like many men who act in haste and then have time to reflect, Herod found holiness and prophecy compelling. John fascinated him. Verse 20 may sound paradoxical, but it makes good psychological sense: Herod was afraid of John, knowing that he was a just and holy man (so unlike the people he normally associated with!); so he kept him safe and used to have him in and let him talk. 'What he heard', says Mark, 'disturbed him greatly, and yet he enjoyed listening to him.' That sounds like genuine court gossip to me; we can imagine the servants shaking their heads and saying, 'Don't know why he still asks for John – he always upsets him,' and 'Well, maybe, but he really enjoys listening to him. Must be a treat to hear someone telling the truth for once.' And so on.

Until the fateful day. Here Mark is a little more coy: he only says that Herodias's daughter 'came in and danced'. But granted the reaction of Herod and his guests (all male, of course), we may imagine that she wasn't just doing a sedate waltz round the room and back again. One thing leads to another, and, as the ancient Greeks knew, the twin forces of *eros* and *thanatos* – sex and death – seem to be all too close to each other. Herod loses his head, metaphorically speaking, and John loses his, literally.

Mark has not included this tale just to boost sales of his book. There are at least three jobs that this story is doing at this point within his narrative.

First, it highlights a key moment in Jesus' own public career. It wasn't only grief at the violent death of his cousin, though no doubt that was there as well. The rest of Jesus' family didn't seem to believe in him, and even John had had his doubts, but at least they were both firmly into the business of announcing God's kingdom. John had prepared the way. Now, with him gone, Jesus was out on his own; and he must have seen John's fate as a signpost pointing towards his own. That, no doubt, was what he wanted to ponder when he tried, unsuccessfully as it turned out, to go away for a while with his closest friends (verse 31).

Second, this story, with John's denunciation of Herod's marital arrangements, prepares us for the implications of the discussion in chapter 10 about 'divorce'. This wasn't an abstract question of ethics. Jesus' questioners were trying to get him to say the same kind of thing that John had done, perhaps with the same consequences. In refusing, Jesus nevertheless managed to give some extremely clear and crisp teaching on marriage, which to this day slices through sloppy and self-serving 'thinking' with the sharp knife of a genuinely creational message: this is how God made us, this is how we should be (10.2–12).

Third, Mark is contrasting the genuine kingdom-work of Jesus and his followers (verses 7–13) with the horrible parody of 'kingdom' you could find then, and can still find, in the palaces of the irresponsible rich, where women are cheap and human life even cheaper. Some people think Mark has written up this story so as to place all the blame not on Herod, but on his wife and stepdaughter. Poor old Herod – led on by a seductive dancer and outwitted by a scheming, vengeful spouse! But this misses the point. Herod remained in charge. His father hadn't stopped at killing his own wife if she offended him, and he himself hadn't stopped at divorcing his previous wife when he tired of her. Herod could do what he wanted. He is the villain here all right.

And he shows, in all its typical gory detail, what the wrong sort of kingdom looks like. Mark allows the story to make its impact, not least to highlight, in the passage that follows, what the true kingdom is like. When he says that Jesus had compassion on the crowds because they were 'like a flock without a shepherd' (verse 34), this is a deliberately pointed comment. There was already an official 'shepherd', that is, a 'king', but he was far too busy ogling women and killing prophets to take any notice of the hungry crowds.

Today

Give us, sovereign Lord, leaders in church and state who will serve your people rather than themselves, and who will listen to the challenge of your word.

WEEK 2: THURSDAY

Mark 6.30–44

[30]The apostles came back to Jesus and told him all they had done and taught. [31]'All right,' he said, 'it's time for a break. Come away, just you, and we'll go somewhere lonely and private.' (Crowds of people were coming and going and they didn't even have time to eat.)

[32]So they went off privately in the boat to a deserted spot. [33]And . . . crowds saw them going, realized what was happening, hurried on foot from all the towns, and arrived there first. [34]When Jesus got out of the boat he saw the huge crowd, and was deeply sorry for them, because they were like a flock without a shepherd. So he started to teach them many things.

[35]It was already getting late when his disciples came to him and said, 'Look: there's nothing here. It's getting late. [36]Send them away. They need to go off into the countryside and the villages and buy themselves some food.'

[37]'Why don't you give them something?' Jesus replied.

'Are you suggesting', they asked, 'that we should go and spend two hundred dinars and get food for this lot?'

[38]'Well,' said Jesus, 'how many loaves have you got? Go and see.'

They found out, and said, 'Five, and a couple of fish.'

[39]Jesus told them to sit everyone down, group by group, on the green grass. [40]So they sat down in companies, by hundreds and by fifties. [41]Then he took the five loaves and the two fishes, looked up to heaven, blessed the bread, broke it, and gave it to his disciples to give to the crowd. Then he divided the two fish for them all. [42]Everyone ate, and had plenty. [43]They picked up the leftovers, and there were twelve baskets of broken pieces, and of the fish.

[44]The number of men who had eaten was five thousand.

The true test of a pastor comes not in the set-piece events (big services, regular fellowship groups, the weekly Bible study) but in the unforeseen, unprepared moments. Especially the ones which, frankly, you not only hadn't planned but hadn't wanted. You are just settling down at last with the newspaper and a cup of tea. You have taken two funerals; you have visited a parishioner who's just had a serious operation; you have organized the rotas for the next few Sundays; and you've even written a careful couple of letters to the leaders of your denomination warning them about the effects of the new church policy on your congregation. A good day's work.

We all know what happens next – though we always wish it wouldn't. The doorbell (if it was the phone, the automatic answering machine could cope for the time being). It's obvious you're in; the lights are on. No escape. You go to the door. There they stand. Perhaps it's the young couple whose baby has just been run over and is in hospital; or the immigrant family threatened with deportation; or the teenager who's just discovered she's pregnant; or the old man still devastated by his wife's death two months ago. You name it. Sheep without a shepherd. This wasn't how you'd planned the evening, but you don't have a choice. And, in any case, you feel . . . sorry for them. Compassion.

It happened to Jesus, too. 'Time for a break,' he had said. 'Come away, just you, and we'll go somewhere lonely and private.' As if. The crowds got there first. I take considerable comfort from knowing that even Jesus could be caught out on this kind of thing. But what came out of him when faced with this disruption to his plans was what always filled him. He was sorry for them. Compassion.

Not only that, but he could find himself, with his friends, quite unprepared for other basic things as well. Five loaves among five thousand people! And they themselves hadn't had time to eat (verse 31). The crowds, meanwhile, had been so excited at the prospect of catching up with Jesus that they hadn't thought about mundane issues like that, either. As someone who likes to plan ahead, especially for events involving a lot of people, I find myself cheerfully horrified at this apparent complete lack of planning and forethought. This wasn't just the law of unintended consequences. This was the law of no imagined consequences at all. Quite irresponsible, in fact.

All right; they could have gone off to the villages, as the disciples proposed (verse 36). But Jesus had been teaching them about the kingdom of God. God's kingdom means the renewal of the world. New creation, full of justice and joy and abundance and hope. For everybody. So what sort of a signal does it send if you spend an hour or two telling people about all the wonderful things God is starting to do for those who follow the new way, but then when it comes down to the serious business of eating tell them to go and fend for themselves? So Jesus decides to put into action the message he's been explaining.

But first, get them all to sit down. I don't think this was just for the sake of orderliness, and I don't think Mark mentions the companies of hundreds and fifties simply in order to explain how it was that they knew, afterwards, how many people had been there. There is a hint of something a bit more organized; something a bit more like . . . well, like someone marshalling troops. Or organizing a community. Or starting a movement. Or something which was a bit like all of those but a bit different too. I think that's what Mark is indicating.

Then the moment. By the time Mark was writing it would have been impossible for any Christian, reading this, not to think of the action they all knew so well, with someone taking bread, giving thanks to God, blessing it, breaking it, and giving it out. The early church saw the Last Supper as the kind of explosive climax to the sequence of meals Jesus had had with them all along, not least these extraordinary feedings out in the lonely countryside. And they saw these meals, and the frequent celebrations of Jesus with his friends, as balanced by the sharing of meals they enjoyed in the early church, where (because they lived as an extended family) it mattered rather a lot that the food was properly distributed.

Some people, indeed, making these connections, have tried to tone down the remarkable multiplication of loaves and fishes. Perhaps, they have said, Jesus showed that one person was prepared to share his picnic, and that made everyone else loosen up and be generous with the food they had brought, too. That has the nice ring of 'Jesus teaching us all to share', which is a good Sunday school lesson (and important for adults too) but hardly the point of Mark's story. Mark's point is that, in God's kingdom, there is indeed a new creation, bursting out in all directions. The generosity of spirit that made Jesus react with sympathy and compassion when the crowds invaded his quiet, private time alone with his friends is the same generosity of spirit that we associate with God, the creator. And since everything we know about God we know most securely because of Jesus, it shouldn't surprise us that sometimes, always surprisingly but always characteristically, Jesus does what God does, providing richly for those who have come to be with him. Even when they'd crashed in on his evening off.

Today

Help us, generous Lord, to trust you to provide not only for the things we know we need but the things we don't know we need. And help us to be generous and compassionate with those who turn to us for help.

WEEK 2: FRIDAY
Mark 6.45–56; focused on 6.45–52

[45]At once Jesus made his disciples get into the boat and set sail across towards Bethsaida, while he dismissed the crowd. [46]He took his leave of them and went off up the mountain to pray.

⁴⁷When evening came, the boat was in the middle of the sea, and he was alone on the shore. ⁴⁸He saw they were having to work hard at rowing, because the wind was against them; and he came to them, about the fourth watch of the night, walking on the sea. He intended to go past them, ⁴⁹but they saw him walking on the sea and thought it was an apparition. They yelled out; ⁵⁰all of them saw him, and they were scared stiff.

At once he spoke to them.

'Cheer up,' he said, 'it's me. Don't be afraid.'

⁵¹He came up to them and got into the boat, and the wind stopped. They were overwhelmed with astonishment; ⁵²they hadn't understood about the loaves, because their hearts were hardened.

. . . So there we were on the boat, we didn't know why he was in such a hurry that we should get away, and we didn't know where he'd gone now or what he was expecting would happen next. It just seemed that there was quite a sense of excitement after that extraordinary business with the loaves – once people had got over their hunger they started to ask questions, they wanted to know how it had happened, and some were getting very enthusiastic . . . and then Jesus told us to leave at once. The last thing we saw was him heading up into the hills. Probably off to pray again, he's always doing that, wish I knew what he said.

Anyway, we were back to the usual routine, on the boat, taking turns with the sails, though that didn't last long because the wind swung round, unpredictable as ever with all those hills round the lake, and so it was back to the oars again. All right for those who'd always done it for a living, but for the rest of us it's horribly hard work, and you take the skin off your fingers if you don't grip the oar properly, which I never seem to be able to manage. And for most of the time it looks like you're not getting anywhere; watching the landmarks on the shore, we didn't seem to be moving much at all.

Then we realized: night was on the way. Darkness comes quick in the spring. Soon all we could see was a few fires by the shore, probably shepherds I suppose. And there we were, between the black sky and the black waters, nobody saying much now, everybody tired, almost forgetting the ridiculous things we'd just seen, taking turns with the oars, losing track of time but everybody longing for sleep, and . . . *what was that?* Did you see something? Yes, over there! It's – no, it can't be! It must be a ghost! We're being followed! Perhaps we're doomed – perhaps it's an angel of death coming to drown us all . . .

And then the voice. So calm, so natural. Almost as though he was teasing us. Here are we, dropping the oars in fright, and there was he, as though he was out for an afternoon stroll, going to walk right by us. And then, 'Cheer up, it's me!' Like, what's the problem?

I wanted to say, 'What d'you mean, "cheer up"? I've lived by this lake all my life and this is the first time I've ever seen anyone walking on it. What's going on? Perhaps we're all mad, or perhaps the whole world has gone mad, or perhaps . . .' But now he's speaking again, and this time I sense that he's looking straight at me, funny how he makes you feel like that.

'Don't be afraid.'

Well, why not, I thought. Anyone in my position . . . and then it happened. Like it sometimes does when he speaks to you. Like a cold drink on a hot day. 'Don't be afraid.' He says that quite a lot, and it rings bells with things I've heard in synagogue. In the scriptures. Angels say it to people. God says it sometimes, too. Now he's saying it.

It was all a bit too much. I simply couldn't put it all together. The healings, the parties, those lawyers getting stroppy with him, then his cousin being killed, then that business with the loaves, and now this. Maybe we *are* all crazy. Maybe we're all going to die if we follow him. But I've never known anybody like him and nor has anybody I know. And when we all went off to his cousin, down by the Jordan, John seemed pretty clear that Jesus was the one.

I'll tell you what, though. I'd rather row across the lake in a storm when he tells me to than do what that jumped-up 'king' up the road would like us to do. I always had a picture in my mind of what the ideal king would look like, and though Jesus isn't at all like that, Herod certainly isn't and could never be. And in fact I have a sense that Jesus is trying to be a different sort of king . . . and it's very appealing, his sort of kingdom, even though I still don't see how it all works out.

Perhaps this is how it's always going to be, for anyone who wants to follow Jesus, now or at any time. Perhaps what he wants from us is not that we should be able to explain it all but that we should just be clear we're going to go on following him. I may not be the sharpest tool in the box (my father always used to say that, because he was a carpenter too, like Jesus' father), but I reckon I'm in this for the long haul. I may not always understand it first time off, but I'll still show up. Or my name's not Thomas Didymus . . .

Today

Surprise us, loving Lord, with your unexpected power and presence, and help us not to be afraid when you do new things in our lives.

WEEK 2: SATURDAY

John 2.13–22

[13]It was nearly time for the Judaean Passover, and Jesus went up to Jerusalem.

[14]In the Temple he found people selling cows, sheep and doves, and the money-changers sitting there. [15]He made a whip out of cords and drove them all out of the Temple, sheep, cows and all. He spilt the money-changers' coins onto the ground, and knocked over their tables.

[16]'Take these things away!' he said to the people selling doves. 'You mustn't turn my father's house into a market!'

[17]His disciples remembered that it was written, 'The zeal of your house has eaten me up.'

[18]The Judaeans had this response for him.

'What sign are you going to show us', they said, 'to explain why you're doing this?'

[19]'Destroy this Temple,' replied Jesus, 'and I'll raise it up in three days.'

[20]'It's taken forty-six years to build this Temple,' responded the Judaeans, 'and are you going to raise it up in three days?' [21]But he was speaking about the 'temple' of his body. [22]So when he was raised from the dead, his disciples remembered that he had said this, and they believed the Bible and the word which Jesus had spoken.

I checked my watch once more, and looked again in my diary. Yes: this was indeed the place we had agreed to meet. And this really was the time we had set. But where was my guest?

It was only then that I noticed a man standing on the far side of the station platform, looking as though he, too, was waiting for someone. But surely . . . I had been imagining someone much older. He was, after all, a highly respected scientist, come to address a student society. I had envisaged a dark suit or coat, a discreet tie, greying hair, perhaps a briefcase. Instead, this man was wearing jeans and a sweater, and was carrying a plastic shopping bag.

He caught my eye. 'You're not . . . ?' Yes; it was him. The place was right, the time was spot on. It was only my expectations that were out of line. We had a great evening.

This was the place: Jerusalem, and the Temple. This was the time: Passover. But they certainly weren't expecting anyone like Jesus. And they certainly weren't expecting anyone to *behave* like Jesus. The Temple was, after all, the Temple. It wasn't just (as people today sometimes wrongly imagine) like a large church on a street corner. It was the centre of everything; the centre, they believed, of the whole world.

More: it was the place where heaven and earth met, joined up, did business. The ancient Jews didn't think of heaven (God's space) and earth (our space) in the way we often do, as two quite distinct places, completely separate and detached from one another. They thought of them as different, all right, but made to be joined together. That's how it had been at the beginning, when 'God made the heavens and the earth', and seemed to be at home in either, or in both together. That's how it had been when, at the end of the book of Exodus, Moses and his skilled workmen had finally constructed the Tabernacle as the place where God would come to meet with his people. And the Jerusalem Temple, as everyone knew, was the descendant of that Tabernacle. David had planned it, Solomon had built it . . .

. . . and the Messiah would one day come to it, great David's greater Son. Only, it was assumed, he would come to defend it, to build it to an even greater splendour, to celebrate it as the place where God would live with his people and make them the greatest nation on earth. And when more appropriate for him to come than Passover time, when the whole nation came to Jerusalem for the great festival, came to celebrate the Exodus from Egypt, the time when God had been with his people in the pillar of cloud by day and fire by night, protecting them, leading them home to their promised land . . .

Jesus took that picture and blew a hole in it big enough to drive cows and sheep through. In fact, that's what he did: drove the cows and sheep, and those who were buying and selling them, out of the Temple altogether. This was, to put it mildly, a problem (as was his knocking over the money-changers' tables, though I bet there were some bystanders who smirked to see those old swindlers scrabbling on the ground for their small change). The Temple was, after all, the place of sacrifice, and most people coming from any distance to offer sacrifice would need to buy the right sort of animals on site. To do that they would need the proper coinage. So Jesus, by driving them all away, was for a moment – but a deeply powerful, symbolic moment – denying the Temple its normal function. The steady stream of sacrifices came to a shuddering halt. The last time that had happened was when the hated Syrians had overrun the place, two hundred years before, and had turned it into a pagan shrine. Now here was someone claiming to be speaking for God and his kingdom – and stopping the Temple from functioning. What sense could that possibly make?

The only explanation Jesus gave was equally cryptic. 'Destroy this Temple, and I'll raise it up in three days.'

As so often in John's gospel, this launches his hearers into a classic misunderstanding. They think, naturally enough, that he's talking about the Temple itself, the building that Herod the Great began to rebuild and which, forty-six years later, was nearly finished. (It was finally completed in AD 63, a mere seven years before the Romans burnt it down for good.) But Jesus wasn't speaking about the building. He was speaking, as John explains, *about his body.*

His body? Yes. At the heart of John's gospel stands the claim, which blows a gaping hole not only in the old Temple but in most modern-day understandings of the very words 'God' and 'human' – the claim that Jesus was, as it were, the Temple in person. He was the place where heaven and earth met, once and for all and completely. He was the place of sacrifice, the place where God would provide the lamb to take away the sins of the world, the reality to which Passover and all that it meant was simply one of the greatest advance signposts.

Once you hold all that together in your mind, John is saying, all the old scriptures come to life in a new way. John quotes one of them, about the zeal for God's house (verse 17, quoting Psalm 69.9, in a context of great suffering). John will introduce his readers to others in due course. But the point is that not just a few odd texts, but the whole sweep of scripture, comes rushing together at this moment, at this place. This wasn't what anybody had expected. But the place was right, the time was spot on, and Jesus had come to do what God had promised: to judge and to save, to sort things out once and for all, to bring heaven and earth together at last.

All this is striking enough, and hard enough for many people today to get their heads around. But there is more. Later in the gospel, and in Paul as well, we are told in no uncertain terms that when the spirit comes we, too, the followers of Jesus, are to be the extension of this new Temple. And that blows a large hole in most people's ideas of what being a Christian might be all about.

Today

Teach us, Lord Jesus, what it meant for you, and what it means for us, to live at the place where heaven and earth meet, and to be ready for the time when you want us to act.

WEEK 3: SUNDAY

Psalm 19

[1]The heavens are telling the glory of God;
    and the firmament proclaims his handiwork.
[2]Day to day pours forth speech,
    and night to night declares knowledge.
[3]There is no speech, nor are there words;
    their voice is not heard;
[4]yet their voice goes out through all the earth,
    and their words to the end of the world.

In the heavens he has set a tent for the sun,
[5]which comes out like a bridegroom from his wedding canopy,
    and like a strong man runs its course with joy.
[6]Its rising is from the end of the heavens,
    and its circuit to the end of them;
    and nothing is hidden from its heat.

[7]The law of the LORD is perfect,
    reviving the soul;
the decrees of the LORD are sure,
    making wise the simple;
[8]the precepts of the LORD are right,
    rejoicing the heart;
the commandment of the LORD is clear,
    enlightening the eyes;
[9]the fear of the LORD is pure,
    enduring for ever;
the ordinances of the LORD are true
    and righteous altogether.
[10]More to be desired are they than gold,
    even much fine gold;
sweeter also than honey,
    and drippings of the honeycomb.

[11]Moreover by them is your servant warned;
    in keeping them there is great reward.
[12]But who can detect their errors?
    Clear me from hidden faults.
[13]Keep back your servant also from the insolent;
    do not let them have dominion over me.
Then I shall be blameless,
    and innocent of great transgression.

[14]Let the words of my mouth and the meditation of my heart
    be acceptable to you,
    O LORD, my rock and my redeemer.

A couple of years ago I found myself in New York at the time when the Museum of Modern Art was hosting an exhibition of Claude Monet's 'Waterlily' paintings. I hadn't realized how enormous they were, or just how abstract the shapes and the colours would seem. And I had forgotten – it was a long time since I'd been to an Impressionist exhibition – the extent to which the extraordinarily fine detail of Monet's painting, the individual brushstrokes and tiny little gobbets of paint here and there, were almost incomprehensible when seen close up (you could walk right up to within a few inches of the paintings), but then, when seen from eight or ten feet back, would make the whole thing spring to life, a life you couldn't see when you were too near. The fascinating thing to me, as a writer, was the way in which the painter could not possibly have seen the whole effect while painting the tiny, almost microscopic, sections. Yet he must have had the whole thing in mind all the time. He must have been fully aware of the larger shape, the balance of the whole thing. He must have known (instinctively? Or from painstaking study and practice? Or both?) what effect the tiny details would have when he stepped back again. Perhaps great art is always like that: the power and sweep of the larger imaginative vision, well served by the fastidious attention to detail.

I have that same sense as I stand back and admire this Psalm, which no less a critic than C. S. Lewis described as the finest poem in the world. You can see why. Read it quickly through, and, instead of just thinking about the meaning of the individual words, look at the shape of the whole thing.

The Psalm falls naturally and elegantly into four sections. We begin with the glorious vista of the skies: the great dome whose ever-changing face and colour announces to the whole world that the living God is the great and majestic creator. 'The heavens are telling the glory of God': yes indeed, and it is a peculiar sort of deafness that stops its ears to this resonating voice. That takes us as far as the middle of verse 4.

But then the poem focuses on the central feature of the heavens: the sun. Here it comes, striding up into the eastern sky, marching through to high noon with great power and energy before resolutely dropping down in the west. And the point is in the final line: nothing is hidden from its heat. If the noiseless voice of the heavens reaches to the ends of the earth, the powerful heat of the sun penetrates to its inmost depths. These first two sections make up the first half of the poem.

The meaning of the poem is found in the hinge between its two halves. Standing as they do in deliberate parallel to one another, they proclaim the most basic of Jewish beliefs, the thing that marks out the Judaeo-Christian tradition (with Islam as a sideways variation) from other world-views. The point is that *the creator God is also the God of Israel*, and vice versa. This might seem obvious, but there are many world-views that, if they believe in a creator, assume that this creator must relate equally to all peoples, and many other world-views that assume that creation is a dark, evil place from which the true God would have to rescue them. The shorthand phrase that sums up this central point is: creation and covenant. The two are in perfect balance, and the balance of the poem reflects this exactly.

The second half thus celebrates the special relationship between the creator God and Israel, the 'covenant' whose charter is the law, the Torah. This, too, falls into two subsections. The first (verses 7–10) explores the wonderful and subtle teaching of the Torah, while the second (verses 11–14) applies this to the individual worshipper, the 'I' of the Psalm.

Standing back, we have travelled an enormous distance: from the full sweep of the majestic heavens, with the sun running its course across them, to the finely crafted law of God and its application to the most intimate and secret aspects of human life. In a sense this, too, is balanced, because the more we know about human beings the more we discover that each one is an utterly fascinating world of meaning, a fathomless well of consciousness, imagination, insight and love. And if that is the overall frame of the poem – from the massive outer world to the massive inner world – the inside portions of the poem balance wonderfully as well, from the all-pervasive heat of the sun to the all-pervasive teaching of the Torah.

Now try coming up close and looking at the particular detail. There is much for everyone to explore; I want simply to concentrate on the second half. In verses 7–10 (the celebration of Torah), the poet reflects on every aspect of the law: law itself, then 'decrees', 'precepts', 'commandment', 'fear' (i.e. reverence), and 'ordinances' or 'judgments'. Torah as a whole is designed, he says, to penetrate, like the sun's heat, down into every aspect of the personality: the breathing life itself ('soul'), the understanding mind that needs wisdom, the heart that needs to be cheered up, the eye that needs to see clearly how things stand in the world and which way to go.

Verse 9 introduces a slightly different angle. The 'fear of the Lord' is the overall reverence that the obedient person displays, a reverence that produces an inner purity or cleanness that, because it has been rinsed free from all pollutants, is incorruptible, 'enduring for ever'. And the 'judgments' or 'ordinances' of the Lord are the more public standards and rules by which a society will be well ordered, with justice firmly in place. There is a sense of completeness. Torah, like the sun with its heat, will bring God's life, wisdom, joy, light, purity and justice into the individual and the community.

But it is the individual upon whom the emphasis then falls in the final verses, giving us a fitting place to rest the mind as we journey through Lent. Precisely because the human heart is so deep and many-sided, a wise worshipper reflects in humility that, left to ourselves, we cannot guarantee that God's loving provision has in fact penetrated, like the sun's heat, to every corner of our personality. If there are hidden faults, flaws deep down in our character, they need to be dealt with. If there is residual pride, it must be held firmly in check (verse 13).

The Psalm closes with the verse that I and many other preachers use at the start of sermons, but that should also be applied to the whole of one's life, as a summary of *where* we should be and *who* we should be. The words we speak, and the thoughts deep in our hearts, are the most reliable indicators of who we really are. And our prayer should be, with the Psalmist, that those words and thoughts will be acceptable to God, to the creator and covenant God, the 'rock' (God the creator, the firm ground upon which we stand) and 'redeemer' (God the rescuer, the covenant God, the giver of the law). We who know the creator God in the face of Jesus Christ and the power of his Spirit should have no difficulty in recognizing that both creation and covenant are fulfilled in that great gift, and no hesitation in praying this Psalm, in its full sweep and its tiny details, in gratitude and love to Father, Son and Spirit.

Today

Glory be to the Father, and to the Son, and to the Holy Spirit, creator and redeemer, giver of life and love and wisdom and light.

WEEK 3: MONDAY

Mark 7.1–13

¹The Pharisees gathered round Jesus, together with some legal experts from Jerusalem. ²They saw that some of his disciples were eating their food with unclean (that is, unwashed) hands.

³(The Pharisees, you see – and indeed all the Jews – don't eat unless they first carefully wash their hands. This is to maintain the tradition of the elders. ⁴When they come in from the market, they never eat without washing. There are many other traditions which they keep: washings of cups, pots and bronze dishes.)

⁵Anyway, the Pharisees and legal experts asked Jesus, 'Why don't your disciples follow the tradition of the elders? Why do they eat their food with unwashed hands?'

⁶'Isaiah summed you up just right,' Jesus replied.'Hypocrites, the lot of you! What he said was this:

With their lips this people honour me,
but with their hearts they turn away from me;
⁷all in vain they think to worship me,
all they teach is human commands.

⁸'You abandon God's commands, and keep human tradition! ⁹'So,' he went on, 'you have a fine way of setting aside God's command so as to maintain your tradition. ¹⁰Here's an example:

Moses said, "Honour your father and your mother," and, "Anyone who slanders father or mother should die." [11]But you say, "If someone says to their father or mother, 'What you might get from me – it's Korban!'" (which means, 'given-to-God'), [12]you don't let them do anything else for their father or mother! [13]The net result is that you invalidate God's word through this tradition which you hand on. And there are lots more things like that which you do.'

We were staying in a remote part of Scotland for a holiday. Our hosts, welcoming us, pointed out that we didn't need a key for the door. They never locked it. The risk of intruders or burglars in that part of the world was more or less nil.

I reflected on other places we had stayed over the previous few years. In some parts of London it takes you two or three keys to get into a house – one for the tall, secure outer gate, another for the main front door, then a third for an inner door after that. Taking no chances. In some parts of the country people are building new estates, almost whole villages, which have a secure perimeter fence, and an outer gate which is staffed 24 hours a day.

Some societies and cultures have been like that, too. When we lived in Montreal, the French majority in the province of Quebec were fiercely protective of their culture – hardly surprising, being as it were a French-speaking island in the middle of a massive English-speaking continent. They passed laws to force businesses to use French on their official documents, even when all the people concerned were English speakers. Looking back through history, many embattled peoples have done the equivalent. If your culture is distinct, many people will want to keep it that way, even at the cost, metaphorically speaking, of triple-locking your gates and doors.

That protective locking-in of a way of life is all the more important if the way of life in question has been given by God – which of course the ancient Jews believed theirs had been. They couldn't stop the Greeks and the Romans taking over the running of their country, but they could maintain their own way of life in their villages and homes. This wasn't so much a matter of an official edict enforced by official police. As often in tight-knit and sensitive cultures, self-appointed guardians of public standards – gatekeepers, if you like – sprang up to watch out for anyone compromising or colluding with the paganism of the surrounding world. That's where the Pharisees came in. They were, to that extent, a bit like a 'Neighbourhood Watch' committee, keeping an eye out for danger.

And danger was what they thought they'd spotted. As in many cultures, a sense of the need to protect the community from pollution is reflected in a heightening of the laws and codes of personal purity and hygiene. Obviously a certain amount of hand-washing makes good sense in any culture. But they elevated it to an art form, and did their best to enforce it, more because of what it symbolized than because of a concern for personal health. *And Jesus and his followers chose to ignore the rule.* As with sabbath observance, they cut clean through it.

This raises two issues. First, what is the status of the traditions that the Pharisees were trying to insist upon? Second, what then is the nature of true purity? The present passage focuses on the first, the next one on the second.

In the present passage, Jesus deals with the underlying question: by what right are the Pharisees adding their traditions on top of what scripture itself says? In fact, Jesus counter-attacks: instead of defending himself and his followers against the charge of impurity, he accuses the Pharisees of inventing traditions that actually undermine the law itself. The example he gives is of a neat dodge that excuses a person from financial obligations to parents. Over the generations the Pharisees, and their successors the rabbis, developed a great deal of subtle 'case law', designed to make the official Torah more practical but in some instances, it seems, actually undermining its original intention.

This is a delicate area because, as I have tried to show, the Pharisees' concern was not simply a matter of being 'legalistic', encouraging people to think they could make themselves good enough for God by their 'good works'. That is a much later problem. They were concerned, rather, to defend and preserve the God-given way of life handed down from their ancestors in obedience to God's covenant. (They would have loved Psalm 19, which we studied yesterday.) The problem was, as St Paul would later put it (he having been a Pharisee himself), that they had 'a zeal for God; but it is not based on knowledge' (Romans 10.2). The 'knowledge' in question was the knowledge that came with Jesus, with his announcement of God's kingdom, and with his saving death and resurrection. Something radically new was happening, something through which Israel's deepest calling and tradition was being fulfilled but also, in the process, transformed. The Pharisees, in trying to enforce other layers of tradition as well, were like people discussing the type of horses you should ride to get from London to Edinburgh when the railways had been invented and were offering a far more efficient mode of transport.

That was the basic issue, and we see it again and again in the gospels. It isn't a matter of 'rules and regulations' on the one side and 'anything goes' or 'do your own thing' on the other, as many today wrongly imagine. It was a matter of God's new initiative in and through Jesus. Like someone triumphantly putting the ceiling on the ground floor of the house they're building, this then creates the floor for the next storey. Jesus was declaring, by his actions as well as his words, that the ground floor was complete, and that it was time to start work on the upper floor, not because the ground floor was a failure but because its job was done. And the view from upstairs would, in some respects, be significantly different.

All this is basic to understanding what Jesus was doing, and what Mark is saying. But of course the same issues resonate through church life in every age. Are we paying attention to the foundational principles of our faith? Or are we allowing all kinds of extra traditions to grow up around them, which might actually undermine some of those foundation principles themselves? This is an old problem, but one that every generation needs to address afresh.

Today

Grant us, gracious Lord, the wisdom to discern which of our customs and habits are genuine expressions of our true faith and which are mere human inventions.

WEEK 3: TUESDAY

Mark 7.14–23

[14]Jesus summoned the crowd again.

'Listen to me, all of you,' he said, 'and get this straight. [15]What goes into you from outside can't make you unclean. What makes you unclean is what comes out from inside.'

[17]When they got back into the house, away from the crowd, his disciples asked him about the parable.

[18]'You didn't get it either?' he asked. 'Don't you see that whatever goes into someone from outside can't make them unclean? [19]It doesn't go into the heart; it only goes into the stomach, and then carries on, out down the drain.' (Result: all foods are clean.)

[20]'What makes someone unclean', he went on, 'is what comes out of them. [21]Evil intentions come from inside, out of people's hearts – sexual immorality, theft, murder, [22]adultery, greed, wickedness, treachery, debauchery, envy, slander, pride, stupidity. [23]These evil things all come from inside. They are what make someone unclean.'

I once watched as an angry crowd burnt a Russian flag. Soviet military aircraft had shot down a Korean civilian plane on 1 September 1983, over the Pacific Ocean, on the suspicion that it had been spying. All on board were killed. It was at the height of the cold war, and the plane, which had taken off in the United States, had strayed into Soviet air space, almost certainly because of a computer malfunction. Around the world, not least in the considerable Korean community in Montreal, where I was then living, furious and grieving Koreans gave vent to their feelings. And when there is nobody you can actually attack, burning their flag is a powerfully symbolic way of saying what you think.

Flags are a comparatively modern invention (though ancient armies would carry 'standards' that functioned in the same way). In the ancient world, especially in the ancient Jewish world, there were various badges of identity that had a similar function. When you kept certain customs, you were waving the flag and celebrating your national identity. If someone tried to abolish or stamp out those customs, this felt like a kick in the stomach, much as if they had burnt your flag.

Among the first-century Jewish customs that functioned in this way was the code that determined what you could and couldn't eat (and, though this raises other questions, who you could and couldn't eat it with). The stories of the Maccabaean martyrs from two centuries before had been told and retold: the seven brothers who refused to submit to the Syrian megalomaniac king, Antiochus Epiphanes, who in his efforts to enforce his kind of paganism on the Jews did his best to make Jews abandon their food laws and – the most obvious feature – to eat pork. One noble old man, forced to open his mouth to receive the forbidden food, spat it out again as they tortured him to death. Such stories were plentiful, and served in turn to reinforce the ban. Don't let the side down! Don't side with those who want to destroy our nation and our customs! Don't let them burn the flag!

Only when we have this picture firmly in mind can we appreciate why Jesus had to go into the house, away from the crowd, before he could explain one of his most cryptic sayings. 'What goes into you from the outside can't make you unclean. What makes you unclean is what comes out from inside.' We today are perhaps more used to the distinction between outward, physical things and the inner world of feelings and thoughts. We are also predisposed, in much Western culture, to think of the inner world as more important than the outer. Most first-century Jews didn't readily make that distinction, or that value judgment. For them, the saying was very puzzling.

It was, perhaps, the only way Jesus could address the larger issue raised by the question about hand-washing (verses 2, 5). What's at stake is the issue of purity and impurity; and purity matters because it's one of the key symbols of Judaism. *And Jesus is radically redefining it.* Is he burning the flag? Many people would think so – if they understood what he meant. Even the disciples didn't get it, so he had to explain. Even then he doesn't spell out the full implications, so Mark, writing for a non-Jewish Christian community (as we can tell from his explanatory notes in verses 3–4), has to make it clear, in the bracket at the end of verse 19.

Watch how this works. First, Jesus declares that nothing that goes in through the mouth can make someone genuinely 'unclean' in any deeply significant sense. Second, he explains this a little further: food, of whatever sort, simply goes in at one end and out at the other. This saying, too, is still cryptic, needing (like lots of rabbinic sayings needed) one more move to make it explicit. So, third, Mark adds his extra note. 'Result,' he says: '*all foods are clean.*'

With that, we might think, the flag has been burnt, and with it all chance of Jesus ever being seen in a positive light from within Judaism.

But wait. What's he saying now? He hasn't abolished the distinction between clean and unclean. He hasn't said purity doesn't matter. It's simply that he has a far deeper, far more radical idea of what purity is. Outward purity – washing the hands, not eating certain foods – is simply a signpost to the real thing. Don't mistake the signpost, he is saying, for the reality. I've come to give you the reality.

Has he? But how? Surely what he's now saying is very bad news indeed. 'What makes someone unclean is what comes out of them, out of people's hearts.' He lists the things he has in mind, and a sad, sordid array it makes. Immorality, theft, murder, greed, envy and the rest. This isn't a liberalizing tendency, as some imagine ('Hurrah! Jesus has got rid of those stupid old rules!'). This is the ultimate standard. God always wanted humans to be genuine humans; greed, pride and the other things corrupt and destroy that genuine humanness (as we all know if we stop to think about it for a minute). If Jesus had simply said, 'Well, no more rules – do what comes naturally,' what we would have 'done naturally' is, alas, a lot of those things: adultery, treachery, and so on.

So what follows from this? Everything we know about Jesus indicates that he doesn't want to leave it there. He isn't telling his disciples all this just to make them – and all the rest of us – feel guilty. He is hinting at something more than diagnosis. He believes he has the treatment we require. He has a cure for the impure heart. He is setting an absolute standard, and providing the means by which, to our amazement, we are to attain it.

Has he burnt the flag? Actually, no. Change the picture. He has taken down the signposts that point to purity. And he has put up, in their place, a new sign, which indicates that Purity itself has arrived.

This (of course) raises all kinds of problems for us. Every pastor – every honest Christian! – knows the failings and impurities that still lurk within. But Jesus' first followers were equally uncompromising. These things must be put to death. And because of Jesus they can be.

Today

Give us courage, gracious Lord, to follow you, this Lent and always, on the path that leads to full purity of heart.

WEEK 3: WEDNESDAY
Mark 7.24–37; focused on 7.24–30

²⁴Jesus got up, left that place, and went to the region of Tyre. When he took up residence in a house, he didn't want anyone to know, but it wasn't possible for him to remain hidden. ²⁵On the contrary: news of him at once reached a woman who had a young daughter with an unclean spirit. She came and threw herself down at his feet. ²⁶She was Greek, a Syrophoenician by race; and she asked him to cast the demon out of her daughter.

²⁷'Let the children eat what they want first,' Jesus replied. 'It's not right to take the children's bread and throw it to the dogs.'

²⁸'Well, Master,' she said, 'even the dogs under the table eat the crumbs that the children drop.'

²⁹'Well said!' replied Jesus. 'Off you go; the demon has left your daughter.'

³⁰So she went home, and found the child lying on the bed, and the demon gone.

He went to the door of the restaurant and looked in. Then he came back to the car, shaking his head. 'It's not our sort of place,' he said. The other occupants of the car understood. They drove on to another part of town, to try their luck elsewhere.

When you heard that story, what did you think? That the phrase 'not our sort' meant 'they're up-market, nose-in-the-air, money-to-burn sort of people – they would think they're too good for the likes of us'? Or did you think he meant 'they're a scruffy, uncouth lot, too loud and rude and rough – they would think we're too "posh" (and we would agree!)'?

Or did you think, perhaps, that it meant, 'most of the people in there are black, and we of course are white' – or perhaps the other way round?

One way or another, almost all human beings find that they're comfortable with certain types of people, people (usually) pretty much like themselves: similar background, culture, habits and so on. This is natural and normal. The question is, what should we do when we're at a boundary? How should we behave towards people who are significantly different from us?

Ancient Judaism presents a special case of this problem. The Jews were very conscious of their status as God's chosen people. Years – centuries, actually – of being hated, persecuted, overrun, sneered at and generally ill-treated by the rest of the world had hardened their sense of God's choice into a solid wall, an invisible steel fence around their national identity. Foreigners were off limits. You could, perhaps, do business with them, but you shouldn't eat with them. Stricter Jews wouldn't even go into non-Jewish houses.

And the strangest thing about this present story is that, to begin with at least, it looks as though Jesus is sharing this viewpoint (call it a 'prejudice' if you like, but prejudices are attitudes you haven't thought about, and they certainly thought this one out very carefully). 'It's not right', he said to the non-Jewish woman, 'to take the children's bread and throw it to the dogs.' Dogs! Yes: that's a word Jews regularly used to refer to non-Jews. And dogs in the ancient world, we must remember, were not family pets. They were rough, often rabid, scavengers. Our equivalent might be 'rats'. (The 'dogs under the table' in the woman's reply are animals that have come in off the street.)

So what was going on? Why on earth did Jesus seem to share this (to us) unpleasant viewpoint?

The answer, unusually for a gospel question, is provided by St Paul. In summing up the argument of his greatest letter, he declares that God's plan in sending the Messiah was a plan conceived in two quite distinct stages. First, the Messiah had to come to God's ancient people, Israel. They had to hear the message of the kingdom. But then, as the ancient prophets and Psalms had often declared, once God had fulfilled his promises to Israel in sending their king, then – and only then! – the non-Jewish nations would be brought in. This is how he puts it: 'The Messiah became a servant of the circumcised people in order to demonstrate the truthfulness of God – that is, to confirm the promises to the patriarchs, and to bring the nations to praise God for his mercy' (Romans 15.8–9). First the Jews, then the Gentiles. Even Paul, who celebrated his own calling as 'apostle to the Gentiles', knew very well that he was part of Phase Two of the plan, not Phase One.

And Jesus was conscious, here and elsewhere, that his urgent task was to implement Phase One. So when he found himself in non-Jewish territory – perhaps he had gone there deliberately to let the fuss over purity (verses 1–23) quieten down a bit – he did his best to stay hidden. He hadn't come to tell the nations that Israel's God was their king. That would be someone else's job. He had come to tell God's people that God was establishing his long-awaited kingdom through his own work. In any case, until he had completed that work (which for him would not be done until he was 'enthroned' on the cross), the way would not be open for the nations to come in. That's the point Paul makes in Galatians 3.10–14 and Ephesians 2.11–21.

So it isn't the case – as some people have rather absurdly suggested – that Jesus was here simply repeating standard Jewish prejudices and that this Gentile woman shook him out of them with her clever repartee. On the contrary. She affirms the special status of the Jewish people, and accepts that any blessing that will come to non-Jews will be a spill-over from what the one true God is doing for them. And, as with the centurion who showed great faith (Matthew 8.1–13), Jesus is happy to respond. God's plan is going ahead in proper order: but, just as Jesus himself was the central bit of God's future arriving in the present, so the healing of this child was a bit of God's future – the time when the Gentiles would come in – arriving in the present.

That, of course, is what we long for and pray for day by day: that the joy, the justice, the love, the rescuing and restoring power of God's ultimate future would come into our lives ahead of time, right now, today. We learn, in our weakness and continuing frailty, that we can't have it all right away. We still await God's full new creation. But, like the woman, we should pester God to give us, in the present, as much as is possible of that future right now. Lent is a good time to rediscover the habit of persistence in prayer, of not taking an apparent 'no' for a final answer.

Today

Draw us deeper, gracious Lord, into your purposes and your plans, so that we may learn to pray energetically for the good things you have in store for us.

WEEK 3: THURSDAY

Mark 8.1–30; focused on 8.22–30

[22]They arrived at Bethsaida. A blind man was brought to Jesus, and they begged him to touch him. [23]He took his hand, led him off outside the village, and put spittle on his eyes. Then he laid his hands on him, and asked, 'Can you see anything?'

[24]'I can see people,' said the man, peering around, 'but they look like trees walking about.'

[25]Then Jesus laid his hands on him once more. This time he looked hard, and his sight came back: he could see everything clearly. [26]Jesus sent him back home.

'Don't even go into the village,' he said.

[27]Jesus and his disciples came to the villages of Caesarea Philippi. On the way he asked his disciples, 'Who are people saying that I am?'

[28]'John the Baptist,' they said, 'or, some say, Elijah; or, others say, one of the prophets.'

[29]'What about you?' asked Jesus. 'Who do you say I am?'

Peter spoke up. 'You're the Messiah,' he said.

[30]He gave them strict orders not to tell anyone about him.

I have a special memory of this passage, going right back to my university days. I had not been a very good pupil in my English Literature lessons at school. I had not really discovered something that any sensible reader of novels and plays learns early on, namely, that a good writer will use one incident to illuminate another one. The writer won't insult the reader's intelligence by saying, 'so, you see, this bit goes well with that bit', 'this image explains the meaning of that incident'. Good writers use all kinds of imagery to make their various points. But perhaps the best sort of imagery is that which arises naturally and properly within the story itself.

Anyway, I was in my first year of undergraduate study of the New Testament, and one of the commentaries I was reading pointed out the rather obvious feature of this present passage in Mark. The story of Jesus healing the blind man in Bethsaida follows the same pattern as the story of Jesus asking his followers about who they thought he was. Once you see that, you will not only understand what Mark was doing in this passage; you will discover that most good writers do it quite a lot. And this discovery makes reading itself, not just reading the gospels, an exciting and dramatic journey. It opens your eyes.

Which is of course the point . . . because the way Jesus opened the man's eyes was in two stages. First he put spittle on his eyes, laid his hands on him, and asked him if he could see anything. 'I can see people,' the man said, 'but they look like trees walking about.' Halfway there, in other words, but needing a second touch. Then, after that second touch, he could see everything clearly. And Jesus, having led him out of the village in order to do this healing, told him to go back home but not to go into the village itself. For some reason this had to be done in secret, and was supposed to stay in secret.

The parallel between this and what happens next is so close that, if Mark had been a novelist, we would say he had constructed it as a convenient fiction. Jesus takes his disciples away from their normal territory, in the region of Galilee around Capernaum, away up north to the slopes of Mount Hermon. He wants this conversation to be private.

However, their destination is significant too. They go to the group of villages that had been renamed, in recent memory, in honour of Augustus Caesar. It was in the territory of Herod Philip (the brother of Antipas and the first husband of Herodias): hence the name 'Caesarea Philippi', distinguishing it from other towns called 'Caesarea', particularly the one about seventy-five miles away on the Mediterranean coast. This town, in other words, has 'royal' associations, both local (Herod) and global (Caesar). Mark was certainly very conscious of this, and there is every reason to suppose that Jesus was too. If his disciples gave him the answer he wanted, they should be aware just what they were saying.

So, the first question, corresponding to the first touch on the blind man's eyes: 'Who are people saying that I am?' Back comes the answer, reminding us of the people appearing like trees walking around – in other words, halfway there but not yet in clear focus: 'John the Baptist; or, some say, Elijah; or, others say, one of the prophets.' Nice try. Not bad. And this tells us (by the way) quite a bit about the style of Jesus' public career, and the way people perceived it: John, Elijah and the prophets hardly give us an image of 'gentle Jesus, meek and mild'. He was acting with power, and speaking equally powerful warnings.

But then the second question, with Herod and Caesar in the background: 'What about you? Who do you say I am?'

'You're the Messiah,' says Peter.

It comes like a thunderclap, opening the skies with a flash. Mark's reader has known all along, of course, because of the voice at the baptism. But Jesus was so different from the messiahs of popular imagination. He was a healer, not a military leader. He spoke about forgiveness, not revenge. He was challenging and redefining Israel's ancient symbols, not reinforcing them. And yet: the cumulative weight of all that Peter and the others had witnessed spoke for itself, and gathered itself together into one great leap of faith and hope, of utter trust in this strange but compelling man and in the God who had so clearly sent him.

Messiah! Not 'the second person of the Trinity'. That realization would dawn more slowly, as the final layer of disguise was penetrated. Indeed, it has sometimes been possible, in the history of Christianity, for people to hide behind a big dogmatic affirmation ('Jesus is God' or at least 'Jesus is Son of God') and to forget that the whole point of his mission was that in and through his work *God was becoming king,* king of Israel (upstaging all the Herods) and king of the world (displacing all the Caesars then and now). 'Messiah' meant 'king'. And 'king' was fighting talk, in Caesarea Philippi of all places.

No wonder Jesus told them strictly not to tell anybody – just as he had sent the blind man away. He was already the subject of critical comment. The Romans had a well-developed spy system; no doubt the Roman governor already had a file on him. Any gossip about *kingship* would bring serious danger. Perhaps that's why many people in our own day have shied away from the idea, too.

That's the trouble with learning to read. It opens up all kinds of possibilities and new challenges. But isn't that what Lent is supposed to be all about?

Today

Lord Jesus, king of the world, rule in our hearts, our countries, our world with the healing power of your love.

WEEK 3: FRIDAY
Mark 9.2–29; focused on 9.2–13

²A week later, Jesus took Peter, James and John away by themselves, and went up a high mountain. There he was trans-

formed before their eyes. ³His clothes shone with a whiteness that no laundry on earth could match. ⁴Elijah appeared to them, and Moses too, and they were talking with Jesus.

⁵'Teacher,' said Peter as he saw this, 'it's great to be here! I tell you what – we'll make three shelters, one for you, one for Moses and one for Elijah!' ⁶(He didn't know what to say; they were terrified.)

⁷Then a cloud overshadowed them, and a voice came out of the cloud: 'This is my son, the one I love. Listen to him!'

⁸Then, quite suddenly, they looked round and saw nobody there any more, only Jesus with them.

⁹As they came down the mountain, Jesus instructed them not to talk to anyone about what they had seen, 'until', he said, 'the son of man has been raised from the dead'. ¹⁰They held on to this saying among themselves, puzzling about what this 'rising from the dead' might mean.

¹¹'Why then', they asked him, 'do the legal experts say "Elijah must come first"?'

¹²'Elijah does come first,' he replied, 'and his job is to put everything straight. But what do you think it means that "the son of man must suffer many things and be treated with contempt"? ¹³Actually, listen to this: Elijah has already come, and they did to him whatever they wanted. That's what scripture said about him.'

The first time I went on live radio, I wasn't conscious of being terrified until I began to speak. Even then, I didn't feel it as a flutter in the stomach, or my knees knocking together, or anything like that. It came out – well, it came out in the words that came out of my mouth. For two or three sentences I heard my voice saying things I hadn't planned, some of which weren't even true. I gradually managed to get hold of my voice – that's what it felt like – and reconnected it to the thinking bit of my brain instead of the panicking bit.

That was a long time ago, but it left a clear impression in my memory, and in my understanding of how the tongue can blurt out odd things under pressure. I imagine that's how it was for Peter, too, when his tongue disconnected from his brain for a moment in the face of one of the most extraordinary sights described anywhere in the Bible, or most other books for that matter.

Of course, what he blurted out wasn't complete nonsense, even though Mark apologizes for him, explaining in verse 6 that he was so terrified he didn't know what he was saying. The idea of building 'shelters' wasn't a reflection of the fact that it would be cold and dark before too long and that somehow Jesus, Elijah and Moses would need somewhere to stay. The 'shelters' were an echo of the ancient Israelite custom of living in makeshift shelters, 'booths' or 'tabernacles', as part of one of the festivals that commemorated the Exodus from Egypt. So perhaps the connection in Peter's frightened, muddled mind was a realization that this was one of those great God-moments, like the time when Moses went up the mountain and came down with his face shining from talking with God . . .

And now here is Moses, once more, but also Elijah, the great prophet who also met God on the mountain. And they are talking with Jesus. And all three are shining, faces, clothes, the lot, described by Mark with another nice touch (people have often suggested that this must be a reflection of Peter's own reminiscences): no laundry on earth could get clothes as white as that. From time to time in the long history of spiritual experiences people have described incidents such as this, but in the present case it's so unexpected, so out of character with everything else even in the gospels themselves, that we are right to be as shocked as the disciples were. What does it mean?

The meaning seems to be a confirmation of all that has gone before at the end of chapter 8. Yes, Jesus really is the Messiah. Yes, the path he is now treading – the path that will lead to the cross – really is the right, God-given way by which he must come into his kingdom, by which he will be obedient to the plan of the one who addresses him, as at the baptism, as his beloved son (verse 7). And yes, all this is happening not as an odd or bizarre occurrence, detached from the long and noble tradition of the prophets and the law, but entirely in line with Elijah and with Moses himself. And yes: looming up behind all of this, making sense of it all but a sense so overwhelming that anyone might find themselves talking nonsense at the glimpse of it all, is the fact that the one of whom the voice from heaven speaks is not just 'my son, the one I love' in a kind of honorific way, a title conveniently bestowed on a mere mortal. The one who is 'son of God' in the sense of 'Messiah' is also 'son of God' in a sense never before imagined, a sense that would take hundreds of years of prayerful thought to begin to understand.

That is the meaning of the discussion, as they come down the mountain, about 'Elijah coming first'. According to Malachi 4, God will send the prophet Elijah back to the people to prepare them for – for what? For *his own coming.* As in Malachi 3.1, the messenger prepares the way for YHWH himself, Israel's God, to return to his people. What the disciples still can't get their minds around is the possibility that the living God might come back in and as a human being, in and as this Jesus they have been following, the Jesus they have just declared to be God's Messiah. But Elijah has already come and gone; Jesus was referring, of course, to John the Baptist. The one who now comes is Israel's Messiah, and more than Israel's Messiah.

Some Christian traditions have done their best to screen out the notion of transfiguration altogether: just a fantasy, they think, a projection of a deeply felt spirituality. Others, such as the Eastern Orthodox churches, have gone the other way, and have insisted that if God's own spirit is at work in his people then we ought to expect transformation, transfiguration, to be taking place in all kinds of ways. It will be unexpected, of course, but in the Christian life we are taught to expect the unexpected. It will be incomprehensible, even, just as the disciples found Jesus' command not to tell anyone until he had risen from the dead. But if we discovered a faith with nothing unexpected or incomprehensible, nothing to shake us from our cosy normal existence and assumptions, we could be fairly sure that it wasn't the real thing.

Today

Let the light of your presence, gracious Lord, shine upon us, and through us, that your love may illuminate the dark places of our lives, and of the whole world.

WEEK 3: SATURDAY
John 3.14–21

[14]'So, just as Moses lifted up the snake in the desert, in the same way the son of man must be lifted up, [15]so that everyone who believes in him may share in the life of God's new age. [16]This, you see, is how much God loved the world: enough to give his only, special son, so that everyone who believes in him should not be lost but should share in the life of God's new age. [17]After all, God didn't send the son into the world to condemn the world, but so that the world could be saved by him.

[18]'Anyone who believes in him is not condemned. But anyone who doesn't believe is condemned already, because they didn't believe in the name of God's only, special son. [19]And this is the condemnation: that light has come into the world, and people loved darkness rather than light, because what they were doing was evil. [20]For everyone who does evil hates the light; people like that don't come to the light, in case their deeds get shown up and reproved. [21]But people who do the truth come to the light, so that it can become clear that what they have done has been done in God.'

I sat for two hours with a young man who could not believe in God's love.

When I say 'could not', that is quite literally how it seemed. He could not believe in God's love in much the same way that he was physically incapable of running a mile in three minutes or lifting a car off the ground with his bare hands. It wasn't that he couldn't understand what I was saying. Nor had he thought through a set of logical arguments that demonstrated to his mental satisfaction that either there wasn't a God or, if there was, he couldn't be a God of love. It was – with the distressing predictability that clergy and counsellors know only too well – that deep down in his memory and imagination there was a sense of unlovedness: of family and teachers telling him he was no good; of never being praised or cherished or celebrated. No doubt there was praise and celebration at various times. But the abiding, life-forming memories are of condemnation, criticism, put-downs. Being made to feel inferior, stupid, weak. So the capacity to receive love, to feel love, to understand love, had been covered over as though with a thick, calloused, leathery skin.

Perhaps we need to think into that sad, depressing frame of mind in order to hear again, with full force, words that have become so well known that they are in danger of forming part of a Christian's mental wallpaper, the pattern so familiar that we no longer notice it. *This is how much God loved the world*, writes John, *enough to give his only, special son*. After all, he goes on, God didn't send the son into the world to condemn the world, but so that the world could be saved by him.

How difficult it is to get the balance right. 'On the cross, when Jesus died,' goes the hymn, 'the wrath of God was satisfied.' I used to say to my clergy that I would only let them sing that line if, every second time they sang the hymn (and some churches sing it an awful lot), they sang 'the *love* of God was satisfied'. God's wrath, properly, is an aspect of his love: it is because God loves human beings with a steady, unquenchable passion that he hated Apartheid, that he hates torture and cluster bombs, that he loathes slavery, that his wrath is relentless against the rich who oppress the poor. If God is not wrathful against these and so many other distortions of our human vocation, he is not loving. And it is his *love*, determining to deal with that nasty, insidious, vicious, soul-destroying evil, that causes him to send his only, special son.

But how does the sending of the son deal with evil? Isn't it just a futile, grandiose gesture? John's whole gospel is his large-scale answer to this question, and unless we read the entire book with this in mind we will miss the point. But in the present passage we are given a single, very cryptic clue. 'Just as Moses lifted up the snake in the desert, in the same way the son of man must be lifted up, so that everyone who believes in him may share in the life of God's new age.' The story is told in Numbers 21. The Israelites grumbled (as they were always doing), and God allowed a plague of poisonous snakes to come and attack them – a deep, evocative symbol of the scaly, slithering discontent of their minds and hearts. As people were dying from the snakebites, God commanded Moses to make a bronze replica of a serpent and put it on a pole, urging the people to look at this uplifted snake and live. (The snake on the pole, in turn, has become a symbol of healing to this day.)

No further explicit explanation is given, in Numbers or by John, as to (so to speak) 'how this worked'. Enough to know that you were at death's door, and that God had provided a remedy. *The* remedy. The present passage is not primarily an exposition of 'atonement theology', but of the faith that grasps, and so is healed by, the God-given, love-given solution to the urgent problem. 'So that everyone who believes . . . everyone who believes . . . anyone who believes . . .' That, clearly, is what John is emphasizing here.

Perhaps that is one of the most important lessons of the Lenten journey. The meaning of the cross will come upon us, like a great shadow into which we must walk, in the days to come. At the moment it is enough to know that we are travelling to the place where we will see Jesus lifted up so that we may escape the condemnation that so many find welling up within the darkness of their own hearts, and which, they fear, may one day be issued by God himself.

But it is God who is saying, in Jesus, 'No! That's not the point! I have sent my son to rescue you from that condemnation!' Yes, it is true: people love darkness rather than light, and don't want to come to the light. Again, every pastor knows that only too well. There's a glorious, beautiful world out there, but some people turn in on themselves, bundling themselves up in darkness to avoid being dazzled. But the God who came into the world in the person of his son, the Word of life, can and will speak his gentle, powerful invitation once more. Come to the light. Look at the son of man, lifted up for you. Think the unthinkable: *this is how much God loved the world*. Believe; trust and share – already, in the present time! – the life of God's new age.

Today

Thank you, Father, for your boundless and lavish love.

WEEK 4: SUNDAY

Psalm 107.1–3, 17–22

¹O give thanks to the LORD, for he is good;
    for his steadfast love endures for ever.
²Let the redeemed of the LORD say so,
    those he redeemed from trouble
³and gathered in from the lands,
    from the east and from the west,
    from the north and from the south.

¹⁷Some were sick through their sinful ways,
    and because of their iniquities endured affliction;
¹⁸they loathed any kind of food,
    and they drew near to the gates of death.
¹⁹Then they cried to the LORD in their trouble,
    and he saved them from their distress;

²⁰he sent out his word and healed them,
  and delivered them from destruction.
²¹Let them thank the Lord for his steadfast love,
  for his wonderful works to humankind.
²²And let them offer thanksgiving sacrifices,
  and tell of his deeds with songs of joy.

Please read the whole Psalm. I know: it's Sunday, you're busy, nine verses is easier than forty-three. But please read it anyway. We live in an age of snippets: the British radio station Classic FM has got big, these last ten years, by playing one movement of this quartet, one segment of this oratorio, one passage from that suite or symphony. Several of the great composers must be permanently turning in their graves: how can you understand the last movement of Sibelius's fifth symphony if you haven't lived through the first two? It's as though you went for a mountain walk and someone gave you a ride most of the way in a helicopter, so that you could simply stride the last half mile to the summit without doing all the work along the way, without coming to terms with the mountain's particular ridges and streams. Anyway, please read the whole Psalm.

When you do, you'll *feel*, as well as see, the obvious pattern. Things are going badly wrong: wandering in the desert, prisoners in darkness, sick and dying, tossed about on the wild ocean. It comes again and again. 'Then they cried to the Lord in their trouble, and he saved them from their distress . . . Let them thank the Lord for his steadfast love, for his wonderful works to humankind.' And then the last ten verses, musing upon it all, and concluding with the invitation to learn wisdom by pondering the whole thing.

Feel the force and sweep of this repeated pattern. Then stand back from it, and hold, within the framework of the Psalm, the different situations you see on the television news, or read about in the newspaper. The different crises and problems you face at work, in your family, in your town. Hunger. Unemployment. Debt. The Middle East. Marriages under threat. Child poverty. And so on. And ask yourself why so few, in today's world, would regard the urgent advice of the Psalmist as anything other than escapism. Today's Western world has labelled 'religion' as either dangerous or irrelevant, and then has wondered why it finds itself wandering in desert wastes, sitting in darkness and gloom, sick and despairing, and tossed to and fro by the wind and the wave.

Because underneath the glorious poetry is glorious theology: the theology of God the creator, God the life-giver, God the rescuer. This is God's world, mysterious though that often seems. Those who find themselves lost and in danger, whether through their own fault or not (some, but not all, of those in trouble in this Psalm had brought it upon themselves), need to shout out to their maker for help. Help will not always come in the way we want or expect. Sometimes it may seem as though nothing has changed. But with that cry for help the world tilts a fraction back towards its proper balance, and ways forward can be found – even though people are then left, as in the last ten verses, to reflect wisely on the larger interconnectedness of human behaviour and the power of God.

The particular passage we are instructed to read today, the first three verses and then verses 17–22, highlight *thankfulness*. Praising God for deliverance is the glad, genuinely human stance which we are invited to take up. And there is special grace and mercy in unexpected places, such as verses 17 and 18. How often do we as pastors hear it said that 'God won't help me because it's my own fault that I'm in this mess'? We sometimes draw back from saying to people 'you brought it on yourself', because that sounds (and sometimes is) cruel. Yet often enough it's true, too. But the good news is, of course, that *while we were still sinners the Messiah died for us* (Romans 5.8). Many of us know this in theory; we all need to be surprised by it in practice, again and again. Yes, some of us need to hear, you are in this mess because you knowingly chose to do this, and this. The warning signs were there and you ignored them. So what? God is the creator, and he is also the rescuer. He takes special delight in rescuing the totally undeserving. When he does that, his love and grace are on display all the more powerfully.

The earliest Christians would have spotted, in verse 20, a clear anticipation of the message of John's gospel. 'He sent out his word and healed them.' 'Your all-powerful word leapt from heaven, from the royal throne, into the midst of the land that was doomed,' wrote the first-century Jewish sage (Wisdom 18.15). A mind steeped in John's Prologue will pick up, of course, the reference to Jesus. But we should also see, in the strange interconnectedness of God's grace, a reference to the healing, rescuing power of the word spoken or written: the word of witness or warning, of comfort or prayer, of challenge or encouragement. Words, after all, reach both heart and mind. And that, again and again, is where healing begins, with thanksgiving as its first fruit.

Today

Be present, merciful and powerful God, to all those who are in despair or desolation this day. May they know your rescuing power, and give you thanks.

WEEK 4: MONDAY

Mark 9.30–50; focused on 9.33–41

[33]They came to Capernaum. When they got into the house he asked them, 'What were you arguing about on the road?'

[34]They said nothing, because on the road they had been arguing about which of them was the greatest.

[35]Jesus sat down and called the Twelve.

'If you want to be first,' he said, 'you must be last of all, and servant of all.' [36]He took a small child, and stood it in the middle of them. Then he hugged the child, and said to them, ³⁷'If anyone welcomes one child like this in my name, they welcome me. And if anyone welcomes me, it isn't me they welcome, but the one who sent me.'

³⁸'Teacher,' said John, 'we saw someone casting out demons in your name. We stopped him, because he wasn't following us.'

³⁹'Don't stop him,' said Jesus. 'No one who does powerful things by my name will be able to say bad things about me soon afterwards. ⁴⁰Anyone who's not against us is on our side. ⁴¹Anyone who even gives you a cup of water in my name, because you belong to the Messiah – I'm telling you the truth, that person won't go unrewarded.'

In the last days of the old regime, the hardest thing for ordinary people in the capital was not knowing who they could trust. The old dictator was still in power, though increasingly weakened by rebellions from inside his country and attacks by forces from outside. But people were still divided. Many couldn't remember a time when he hadn't been their leader; they had always been loyal to him up to now, why should they change? Besides, if there were foreigners attacking the country, shouldn't they stand firm, with proper national pride? But others – often in the same family – were quite clear. The man has to go. We belong to tomorrow's world, we follow the new leaders, we are going to win.

And when you walk out of your front door, you don't know who is going to be on which side. Which conversations will be 'safe', and which will be full of danger? Is this person – this family – this shopkeeper – *is he on our side?* You can see how easily this turns into paranoia. Trust nobody but the tight circle you already know.

And you can see how that, in turn, becomes a kind of superiority complex. We are the true believers, the real revolutionaries, the ones who have seen through the old system and know exactly how the new one should come about. And, within that again, we – just you and I – are at the leading edge of all this.

Even our friends, here in this room, are sometimes muddled. But we are the ones! We see the whole picture! We are . . . well, we mightn't say it in so many words, but we are the greatest!

Utterly natural, and utterly subverted by the very message that Jesus' first followers were supposed to be learning. Of course, they hadn't learnt it; Jesus was trying to explain to them that the kingdom would come through his own death (verses 31–32). But they didn't get it; and the sign that they didn't get it was that they were arguing on the road as to, yes, which of them was 'the greatest'. It's the Muhammad Ali syndrome – except that, latterly at least, the great boxer always made his claim with a grin and a hint of self-deprecating irony. Jesus' followers don't seem to have done irony. But they were now going to get some.

If they don't understand plain speech ('the "son of man" is to be given over into human hands', and so on), maybe they'll understand a symbol. Here is a child. Utterly present in the moment; utterly unconcerned about tomorrow, about status, about hierarchy. (Oh, yes, children can also be walking examples of original sin. Don't romanticize. But don't forget the ironic lesson, either.) What, after all, would 'greatness' in God's kingdom look like? Wouldn't it mean being the sort of person through whom God's powerful presence would become real? Wasn't that what had happened back at the start of chapter 6 when they went out and healed people and announced that God was becoming king?

Well, yes. But if you want to know how God's powerful presence comes most easily into the world, go and welcome a child in Jesus' name. You will be welcoming Jesus himself – and, by doing so, you will be welcoming 'the one who sent me' (verse 37). Here is, as it were, the hot line into the powerful presence of God. It isn't a matter of senior, seasoned leaders going off with their noses in the air and making it all happen. It's a matter of the least of all, the servant of all, being the greatest.

And with that lesson, the other lessons fall into place (though, as we shall see, the disciples were still getting it wrong in the next chapter). Yes, obviously there are enemies out there. There are plenty of people who are deeply suspicious of Jesus' kingdom-movement; they might not like Herod, they might not approve of Caesar, they certainly wouldn't like the chief priests, but they are not at all sure about this strange carpenter from Nazareth with his motley crew of followers. So what are we to do? Be suspicious of everyone except our tight little circle (and even, did they but know it, of some within that)? No.

Suppose there is someone doing powerful works in the name of Jesus. Well, that's what counts. Anybody who discovers just how powerful Jesus' name really is will not be about to turn round and inform on his followers (though such a person had better be careful about using that powerful name, as Acts 19.13–17 reminds us). This passage is a vital warning now, as it was then, about the danger of imagining that God can and will only work through the people 'we know about'. This isn't just a matter of modern denominations. Most churches (thank God!) are increasingly discovering that there are people down the street whom they used to ignore or despise, who do things a little differently from the rest of us, but who are themselves living as active agents of God's love and the power of Jesus.

Yes, there is the opposite warning, too. When there is powerful evil on the rampage, when fierce spiritual warfare is at its height, you may have to be told that 'if you're not with me, you're against me' (Matthew 12.30). Context is all. Here we are talking about the disciples trying to rank themselves, both one against another and, as a group, against 'outsiders'. How can that embody the childlike humility of a group who follow a Master who is going to the cross?

Today

Give us, gracious Lord, the humility to follow wherever you lead, with no thought for our own status except for that of a servant.

WEEK 4: TUESDAY

Mark 10.1–16; focused on 10.1–12

¹Jesus left the region, and went to the districts of Judaea across the Jordan. A large crowd gathered around him, and once more, as his custom was, he taught them.

²Some Pharisees approached him with a question. 'Is it permitted', they asked, 'for a man to divorce his wife?' They said this to trap him.

³'Well,' answered Jesus, 'what did Moses command you?'

⁴'Moses permitted us', they replied, 'to write a notice of separation and so to complete the divorce.'

⁵'He gave you that command', said Jesus, 'because you are hardhearted. ⁶But from the beginning of creation

> male and female he made them; ⁷and that's why
> the man must leave his father and his mother
> and cleave unto his wife; ⁸so that the two
> become one flesh.

'There you are, then: they are no longer two, but one flesh. ⁹What God has joined, humans must not split up.'

¹⁰When they were back indoors, the disciples asked him about this.

¹¹'Anyone who divorces his wife', said Jesus, 'and marries someone else commits adultery against her. ¹²And if she divorces her husband and marries someone else she commits adultery.'

The building inspector hurried across the road to where the workmen had already got the wall a few feet up from the ground.

'What are you doing?' he asked, in some agitation.

'We're building this house!' they replied. 'Do you have a problem with that?'

'Yes, I do!' he said. 'I made it quite clear at the planning stage that the ground here wasn't safe to build on. You need a proper foundation, and this ground won't take it!'

Work stopped while the foreman was called. And then the architect. Then it became clear.

'We figured out what the problem was,' said the architect. 'There was a layer of gravel underneath the foundations, and it was causing slippage. We dug down last week, while you were away, and we've got to solid rock. So we've built up again, and this house is going to be as sound as a bell!'

They had gone down to the foundation. The interim regulations that warned of possible danger could now be set aside, not because they were not right and proper at the time, but because the danger they reflected had been dealt with.

That is the underlying logic of Jesus' answer to the Pharisees. This was, as Mark says, a trick question, trying to trap Jesus (verse 2) – not trying to trap him with 'theological heresy' or any such thing, but with the more obvious snare of political trouble. There they were in 'the districts of Judaea across the Jordan' – in the territory of Herod Antipas, who had imprisoned and then executed John the Baptist for having the temerity to say that he, Herod, should not have divorced his first wife and then married Herodias, who in turn divorced Herod's brother Philip to make the second marriage possible. The Pharisees knew that Jesus was likely to take a strict line, and that an unguarded word from him, suitably reported back to Herod, might do the trick. They would be able to sit back and watch Herod do their dirty work for them.

This explains the two-stage nature of the passage. As in chapter 7, with the contentious issue of clean and unclean food, and as in chapter 4, with the deeply subversive parable of the sower, the seed and the soils, Jesus will say one thing out in the open and something much more pointed and clear back inside the house. If he had said verses 11 and 12 where the Pharisees could hear, a tip-off to Herod would have followed at once.

Instead, Jesus meets their question with one of his own. 'What did Moses command you?' They are, after all, a self-appointed high-octane pressure group, specializing in keeping the ancestral law to the nth degree. They should know.

They quote Deuteronomy (24.1–4). Moses set up an arrangement for how divorce was to be regulated. You couldn't just send a woman away; she had to be given a proper legal document, for her own protection and so that everyone would know how matters stood.

That is how things stood at the time. The foundation was shaky. You couldn't guarantee that the building would stand up. So you had to make alternative arrangements. But Jesus is going down a long way deeper. He agrees that there was indeed a problem to which Moses' solution was the appropriate one at the time. But he is going down to bedrock. 'From the beginning of creation,' he says, 'male and female he made them,' and that's how it's to be: leave, cleave, one flesh. God joins them; humans mustn't split them up.

This too, of course, is an appeal to 'Moses', since the book of Genesis was known as 'the first book of Moses'. Jesus is not over-throwing Moses. He is merely claiming (merely! It's perhaps the biggest implicit claim in the whole book) that with his work, with the launching of God's kingdom, a new creation is under way, a creation in which the original intention can now be fulfilled.

Doesn't that mean he is building on gravel? Are not human hearts still hard? Isn't it cruel to deny people the permission that Moses granted?

No. *Jesus is claiming, by strong implication, that with his kingdom-mission there is a cure for 'hardness of heart'.* To be sure, it isn't a magic cure. It doesn't necessarily work over-night (though there are remarkable cases of dramatic trans-formation). But this, as in chapter 7, is the secret at the very centre of so much that Jesus was doing. His teaching may seem quite unrealistic – to those who still think they are building on the shaky foundation of the hardened human heart.

The church, from very early on, found this quite a challenge, which is why we find the special cases mentioned in Matthew (5.32 and 19.9) and Paul (1 Corinthians 7.15). But these 'exceptions' only serve to highlight the principle. All this makes a nonsense of the still popular idea that the Old Testament is fierce and legalistic and the New Testament is relaxed and easy-going. Not a bit of it. The Old Testament recognizes that, at the present moment, the foundation is not in place, so the house of God's ultimate creation-purposes cannot necessarily stand straight upright. Jesus indicates that, with the coming of God's kingdom, the original intention in creation can be established on the bedrock of God's healing, forgiving love.

It is this that grounds the stern word that Jesus then speaks once they are safely back inside the house. He might have been pointing straight at Herod in verse 11, and at Herodias in verse 12. And he might well be pointing at those who, today, use the caricature of a fierce Old Testament and a kindly, easy-going New Testament as an excuse to get away altogether from God's original creative intention, by whatever means. The challenge for us all is so to follow Jesus, so to get to know him and be transformed by his healing love, that we can be part of that building, that new creation, in whatever way he wills.

Today

Renew our hearts, gracious Lord, by the power of your love and your spirit, that we may live as people of new creation.

WEEK 4: WEDNESDAY

Mark 10.17–31

[17]As he was setting out on the road, a man ran up and knelt down in front of him.

'Good teacher,' he asked. 'What should I do to inherit the life of the Age to Come?'

¹⁸'Why call me "good"?' replied Jesus. 'No one is good except God alone. ¹⁹You know the commandments:

Don't kill.
Don't commit adultery.
Don't steal.
Don't swear falsely.
Don't defraud.
Honour your father and your mother.'

²⁰'Teacher,' he said, 'I've kept all of them since I was little.'

²¹Jesus looked hard at him, and loved him.

'One more thing,' he said. 'Go away, and whatever you possess – sell it, and give it to the poor. You will have treasure in heaven! Then: come and follow me.'

²²At that, his face fell, and he went off sadly. He was very wealthy.

²³Jesus looked slowly around. Then he said to his disciples, 'How difficult it is for the wealthy to enter the kingdom of God!'

²⁴The disciples were astonished at what he was saying. So Jesus repeated once more, 'Children, it's very hard to enter the kingdom of God! ²⁵It would be easier for a camel to go through the eye of a needle than for a rich man to enter God's kingdom.'

²⁶They were totally amazed, and said to each other, 'So who then can be saved?'

²⁷'It's impossible for mortals,' Jesus said, looking hard at them, 'but it's not impossible for God. All things are possible for God.'

²⁸'Look here,' Peter started up, 'we've left everything and followed you.'

²⁹'I'll tell you the truth,' replied Jesus. 'No one who has left a house, or brothers or sisters, or mother or father, or children, or lands, because of me and the gospel, ³⁰will fail to receive back a hundred times more in the Present Age: houses, brothers, sisters, mothers, children, and lands – with persecutions! – and finally the life of the Age to Come. ³¹But plenty of people at the front will end up at the back, and the back at the front.'

'With these binoculars,' said the salesman, taking me outside the shop, 'you can tell the time on the church clock half a mile away. With these ones, though' (his assistant brought him out another pair), 'you can lip-read what the vicar's saying to the people as they come out. And with *these* ones –' (the third and largest pair were produced, monstrously long and weighing several pounds), 'well, these ones bring the church so close you can hear the choir singing.'

A tease, of course, but it set me thinking about the way in which the zoom lens of a camera, or the extraordinary magnification of binoculars, enable you not just to see a bit more clearly what you can see already, but to see new details which give different meaning to the whole picture.

Mark's portrait of the eager young man who ran up and knelt before Jesus has something of that zoom-lens quality. So often, elsewhere in the gospels, we are told what Jesus said but not the way he looked at people, or the emotions that crossed his face. But here – this scene obviously made a deep impression on the disciples as they saw the little sequence unfold – we have three indications which, if you were a theatrical producer putting this on as a play, would enable you to catch the mood, the tension and the drama of the whole thing very well.

To begin with, when the young man declares that he's kept all the commandments since he was little, 'Jesus looked hard at him, and loved him' (verse 21). How does Mark know he loved him? There must have been an extra dimension in that long, hard look. Jesus gazed at the young man and saw in him a real eagerness, a quick readiness to do whatever it took to be part of God's new world (the 'Age to Come' as opposed to the 'Present Age' – see verse 30) when it arrived, as arrive it surely would now Jesus was here. You would have to have a heart of stone not to be moved by such enthusiasm, and Jesus' heart was anything but stony.

But then Jesus dropped the bombshell. One more thing: sell up, give it away, and follow me. 'Costing not less than

everything' was how T. S. Eliot described the challenge of following Jesus, and that's what Jesus was asking now. The enthusiasm
changed to disappointment like a dark cloud suddenly appearing from nowhere to cover the sun. Off he went.

Then the second zoom lens on Jesus: he 'looked slowly
around'. Stand there with the disciples as they watch, hardly
daring to move. What's he going to say? Shouldn't he have
closed the deal, told the young man to come as he was, and
hoped to explain the cost to him more fully as they went on?

In our mind's eye we see that gaze swing round the silent,
watching group. He's reading their faces and they his. Then he
says something which shocks them as much as his challenge
shocked the young man. 'It's difficult for the wealthy to enter
God's kingdom.' They were so astonished that Jesus spells it
out in more detail. Easier for a camel to go through the eye of
a needle, and all that. More amazement.

But why? We are perhaps too used to this element in Jesus'
teaching (not that we have taken it seriously, but we know it's
there). But the disciples lived in a world where wealth was seen
as an index of God's blessing. If rich people couldn't be part of
God's kingdom, then who could?

Once more the zoom lens. 'It's impossible for mortals,' Jesus
said, looking hard at them. Once again we stand silent on
the edge of the crowd, open-mouthed, as his level, steady, sad
gaze meets theirs. Don't they get it yet? Haven't they seen the
point? Didn't they remember the Sermon on the Mount?
God's kingdom doesn't work by the ordinary human rules. All
things are possible to God, but that's just as well because what
needs to happen isn't just difficult; it's impossible. God's kingdom, and the life of the Age to Come, are all about new creation.
You can't generate them from within the present age. You can't
push your way in by trying a bit harder, by making a bit more
money, by impressing God or Jesus with good resolutions or
even great moral achievements. All of these are like someone
climbing up a ladder to try to get to the moon. Forget it.

The vividness of the scene, with these three zoomed-in snapshots of Jesus himself in a critical two-way conversation, part with the young man and part with the disciples, highlights the larger underlying point. In the previous scene, we saw Jesus discussing the question of marriage and divorce, and going back behind the law of Moses to the principles of the original creation. Now we see him going out beyond the law of Moses (which the young man declares he's kept all through) to the principles of God's new creation. God is doing a new thing, and the only way to get there with him is to abandon all pride, all achievement, all status, all possessions. None of them count for a thing.

There will, to be sure, be compensations. There are many Christians who have discovered the truth of verse 30: having left all their own prospects, they have 'homes' in other towns, other lands; they have brothers and sisters all over the place. That, at its best, is how the global community of Jesus' followers really functions. But when God acts he characteristically turns things upside down. The first will be last and the last first.

St Paul discovered the truth of all this. He had, he said, abandoned all his pride of upbringing, training, heritage and so on. He lost it all to gain the Messiah (Philippians 3.2–11). After all, Jesus had 'loved me and gave himself for me' (Galatians 2.20). On the basis of this, some have suggested that Paul was the young man in this story. Utterly fanciful, of course, but it might help us zoom in one more time and ask the question: can you see the look on that young man's face? What would you say to yourself as you stood by, heard what Jesus was saying and watched the way he looked hard, first at the young man, then at his followers?

Today

Give us courage, gracious Lord, to see what's getting in the way of our total commitment to you, and to give it up so that we may share your life, now and always.

101

WEEK 4: THURSDAY

Mark 10.32–45; focused on 10.35–45

[35]James and John, Zebedee's sons, came up to him.

'Teacher,' they said, 'we want you to grant us whatever we ask.'

[36]'What do you want me to do for you?' asked Jesus.

[37]'Grant us,' they said, 'that when you're there in all your glory, one of us will sit at your right, and the other at your left.'

[38]'You don't know what you're asking for!' Jesus replied. 'Can you drink the cup I'm going to drink? Can you receive the baptism I'm going to receive?'

[39]'Yes,' they said, 'we can.'

'Well,' said Jesus, 'you will drink the cup I drink; you will receive the baptism I receive. [40]But sitting at my right hand or my left – that's not up to me. It's been assigned already.'

[41]When the other ten disciples heard, they were angry with James and John. [42]Jesus called them to him.

'You know how it is in the pagan nations,' he said. 'Think how their so-called rulers act. They lord it over their subjects. The high and mighty ones boss the rest around. [43]But that's not how it's going to be with you. Anyone who wants to be great among you must become your servant. [44]Anyone who wants to be first must be everyone's slave. [45]Don't you see? The son of man didn't come to be waited on. He came to be the servant, to give his life "as a ransom for many".'

'Sorry, you can't have that seat. It's already been booked.' I was frustrated. It was one of my favourite train journeys, past some magnificent scenery. But the train was crowded, and there were hardly any seats on the side where one would get the best view. Only one, in fact; and I made for it – to be told it was already reserved. A standard disappointment, whether on trains or planes, or even in the theatre.

But when Jesus told James and John that the places they wanted had already been booked, they must have been puzzled.

What did he mean? They were thinking, of course, of something approaching royal thrones. Jesus would be in the middle, and they would be on either side of him: the Galileans have come to town, Zebedee's boys have made it to the top at last! Now we'll sort things out – especially those people who have been getting in the way, trying to stop Jesus launching his kingdom. We'll show them! (Compare Luke 9.54.) And, who knows? – Jesus wasn't married, so when his time came to pass on, someone would have to take over . . .

Dream on, thunder-boys. You haven't been listening. 'Can you drink the cup I'm going to drink? Can you receive the baptism I'm going to receive?'

Their answer ought to make us gasp. No problem, boss, they say. Of course we can. We're up for anything.

They still don't realize what they're saying. Yes, says Jesus, maybe you will share my cup and my baptism. But sitting at my right and my left . . . and the passage goes on to wider applications.

But stay with the question for a moment. Mark has no doubt what all this refers to. Five chapters later we discover what James and John were asking for, and we shudder. The moment when Mark tells us that Jesus is enthroned in his kingdom – in other words, the moment he tells us that he has the words 'King of the Jews' above his head – he also tells us that they crucified two bandits alongside him, one on his right and one on his left (15.27–28). That not only explains Jesus' reaction to the request of James and John. It also confirms the point that Jesus is now about to make.

Actually, he's been telling them this for the last two chapters, and they still haven't even begun to grasp the point. *He is going to die*; and his death will not be a messy accident, will not simply be the kind of thing that happens to people who lead powerful renewal movements or who go about declaring that God is now becoming king, and acting in accordance with that. His death will be the *means by which* he becomes king, and hence – since the two are intimately bound up with one another – the means by which *God becomes king*. This is how, as he said in 9.1, God's kingdom will come 'with power' – but it is a power that, as Paul saw, is utterly redefined.

The redefinition, in fact, is the point of it all. James and John, like Peter at Caesarea Philippi, are still thinking as humans think rather than thinking as God thinks. Look at the pagan world, says Jesus. (We look around at our own world and – guess what! – remarkably little has changed.) The rulers of the nations lord it over their subjects, and people in positions of power boss other people around. That, no doubt, is what James and John wanted to do, and it's what a great many people in our world long to do. If you can't beat them, join them. But that isn't how things work in the kingdom of God. Back, once again, to the lesson which the disciples had to learn, but still hadn't learnt, after the encounter with the rich young man.

In God's upside-down world (or should it be right-way-up world?) everything is reversed. It's like *Through the Looking Glass*. Anyone who wants to be great must be (what did they expect: 'prepared to work hard' or 'exceptionally prayerful and well behaved' or 'utterly trustworthy and responsible'?) – must be your *servant*. The one who hands you a fresh cup to drink out of. The one who cleans up when you've finished eating. The one who scrapes the mud off your boots when you come in from the field. The one you take for granted, who does the things you can't be bothered to do. Yes: your servant. In fact, anyone who wants to be first must . . . again, what do we expect? 'Must have exceptionally sharp elbows and be prepared to get up very early in the morning to get ahead of all the other pushy people out there'? No: to be first, you must be *slave of all*. Slave! Even lower than 'servant'. The slave has no rights; no human dignity. Nothing to make you envy or look up to him. People despise slaves. Treat them as dirt. Look the other way rather than catch their eye . . .

Yes, precisely. Now watch:

> He had no form or majesty that we should look at him;
>   nothing in his appearance that we should desire him.
> He was despised and rejected by others;
>   a man of suffering and acquainted with infirmity;
>   and as one from whom others hide their faces
>   he was despised, and we held him of no account.

That is the passage (Isaiah 53.2–3) that Jesus had in mind. It goes on to speak of this slave, this 'servant of the Lord', wounded for our transgressions, bruised for our iniquities, receiving in himself the punishment that made us whole (53.5). He will give his life 'a ransom for many' (verse 45, summing up Isaiah 53.10–12).

It isn't just, in other words, that James and John haven't been paying attention to what Jesus has been saying about what will happen to him in Jerusalem. They haven't begun even to glimpse that Jesus' forthcoming death will be the moment when, and the means by which, God's saving power is unveiled in all its glory – through the suffering and death of the 'servant'. In Isaiah, this is how God's kingdom will come (52.7–12). In Mark, too, this is how God's kingdom will come. How it has already come. How its work will continue to be implemented. This is Jesus' powerful, deeply subversive, combination of 'political theology' (verses 42–44) and 'atonement theology' (verse 45). It draws together what much modern thought has split apart, and still holds out an agenda to Jesus' followers which we, like James and John, still find hard to grasp, let alone to live out.

Today

Help us, Lord Jesus, servant and saviour, to be grasped by your vision of God's new world, and to follow you in the servant-work through which it is accomplished.

WEEK 4: FRIDAY

Mark 10.46–52

[46]They came to Jericho. As Jesus, his disciples and a substantial crowd were leaving the town, a blind beggar named Bartimaeus, the son of Timaeus, was sitting by the road. [47]When he heard it was Jesus of Nazareth, he began to shout out: 'Son of David! Jesus! Take pity on me!'

[48]Lots of people told him crossly to be quiet. But he shouted out all the louder, 'Son of David – take pity on me!'

[49]Jesus came to a stop. 'Call him,' he said.

So they called the blind man.

'Cheer up,' they said, 'and get up. He's calling you.'

[50]He flung his cloak aside, jumped up, and came to Jesus.

Jesus saw him coming. [51]'What do you want me to do for you?' he asked.

'Teacher,' the blind man said, 'let me see again.'

[52]'Off you go,' said Jesus. 'Your faith has saved you.' And immediately he saw again, and he followed him on the way.

One of the best sermons I have heard for a long time was an exposition of this passage. It took the theme of the blind man's cloak. The cloak, the preacher pointed out, was the man's security. Shade in summer, warmth in winter, it functioned as the outer shell, like a small tent, in which the few possessions the man had could be kept in such relative security as a blind man could expect.

All the more startling, then, that when they told Bartimaeus that Jesus was calling him, 'he flung his cloak aside', jumped up, and came to Jesus. This stands (so the preacher pointed out) as a signpost to all of us. It takes time, perhaps, for us to acquire enough self-knowledge to see what the 'cloak' is in which we sit, huddled but relatively secure. There may be many things, not just possessions (though those are likely to be high on our lists), which function for us as the cloak functioned for the blind man. And when Jesus calls, the sign that we are ready to do business with him is that we fling it aside. 'It's time to shed the cloak,' the preacher repeated.

But there is another dimension to this story, which we do equally well to ponder as we consider it – as Mark undoubtedly intended us to consider it – as a sharp-edged example of what it's like for all of us as we hear Jesus' call and decide what to do about it. The story has a familiar shape. It begins with an obvious need: here is a blind beggar, asking for money as they did and still do. 'Take pity on me,' is a normal way of saying 'Spare me some small change'. 'Have pity on a blind man!' 'Show me some kindness!' He must have called out those appeals a thousand times, perhaps ten thousand times, a day. A constant litany, only ending when he made his way home, each night, with such coins as generous passers-by had given him.

This time, we must assume, it started out no differently. He'd heard that Jesus was coming; well, 'Son of David', eh? That sounds royal, and where there's royalty there's money. Let's hope for a good day today! 'Son of David – take pity on me!'

What did he expect? That Jesus would tell his money-man to go over and give him something? Perhaps. But Jesus has just told another man that money isn't where it's at. Is that really going to be his response?

Freeze the frame there and come into it yourself. When you get a sense, today, that Jesus is coming by your way, what are you going to ask him for? What are you hoping he'll do for you? What are the normal requests that will bubble up out of your immediate world, the pressures of your life? Money? A better home? Friendship? The repairing of some relationship that's gone horribly wrong? Success in an exam, or an interview? A good job? All sorts of things, no doubt.

But then comes the moment. How easy for Jesus, with pressures of every sort, crowds all round, and knowing what is waiting for him when they leave Jericho and climb the long hill to Jerusalem – how easy for Jesus to deal quickly with this man, and pass on to 'more important' things. But there are no unimportant people in the kingdom of God. Jesus tells them to call him. Bartimaeus flings off the cloak and comes to him.

Then, at last, the crucial moment – for Bartimaeus, and for us, too. 'What do you want me to do for you?' If I were a movie director, I would freeze the frame again at this point, and allow the question to echo as though down a deep well, with pictures flitting to and fro in the man's mind. What do you *want*, really want, me to do?

We might think: well, of course he'll want to be able to see again. But will he? To see again would mean that his livelihood, such as it was, would be gone. No more begging. To ask for his sight would mean not only having the faith that Jesus could and would do it. It would mean having the faith that he could set off on a whole new life, a life set free by Jesus from the prison where it had been kept, but free to do . . . what? A new, strange, dangerous world opened up. How easy for him to back down, to say, 'Teacher, I need money.' Play safe. Don't be extreme, don't build your hopes up. You can feel the voices in his head as Jesus' question echoes around, bounces off the walls of his mind.

No. Say it. Now or never. We've already shed the cloak, now let's go for the big one. 'Teacher, let me see again.' And the dark, deep well with its imaginary pictures turns inside out, and there is the sunlight, and the trees, and people all around, and the cloak lying in a heap across the street, and Jesus standing there, smiling and reaching out his hand, and the people cheering and waving and coming up to congratulate him . . .

'Off you go,' said Jesus. 'Your faith has saved you.' Yes, and that faith is going to be what will continue to save you, because you're going on a journey. Healing isn't the end of the story. It's the start of a new story, the opening up of a new world. Bartimaeus follows Jesus, says Mark, on the way: well, of course he would. 'The way' is one of the slogans the early Christians used for their new movement. Bartimaeus was already on it. Once you really tell Jesus what you really want, and once he really does it for you, you don't have much choice.

Today

Help us, loving Lord, to be absolutely clear with you about our deepest needs, and to trust you to lead us on from there wherever you want.

WEEK 4: SATURDAY

John 12.20–33

²⁰Some Greeks had come up with all the others to worship at the festival. ²¹They went to Philip, who was from Bethsaida in Galilee.

'Sir,' they said, 'we would like to see Jesus.'

²²Philip went and told Andrew, and Andrew and Philip went together to tell Jesus.

²³'The time has come,' said Jesus in reply. 'This is the moment for the son of man to be glorified. ²⁴I'm telling you the solemn truth: unless a grain of wheat falls into the earth and dies, it remains all by itself. If it dies, though, it will produce lots of fruit. ²⁵If you love your life, you'll lose it. If you hate your life in this world, you'll keep it for the life of the coming age.

²⁶'If anyone serves me, they must follow me. Where I am, my servant will be too. If anyone serves me, the father will honour them.

²⁷'Now my heart is troubled,' Jesus went on. 'What am I going to say? "Father, save me from this moment?" No! It was because of this that I came to this moment. ²⁸Father, glorify your name!'

'I have glorified it,' came a voice from heaven, 'and I will glorify it again.'

²⁹'That was thunder!' said the crowd, standing there listening.

'No,' said others. 'It was an angel, talking to him.'

> ³⁰'That voice came for your sake, not mine,' replied Jesus. ³¹'Now comes the judgment of this world! Now this world's ruler is going to be thrown out! ³²And when I've been lifted up from the earth, I will draw all people to myself.'
>
> ³³He said this in order to point to the kind of death he was going to die.

It happens all the time in spy movies and TV thrillers. Someone does or says something which, by itself, seems quite unimportant. But the hero, or perhaps the villain, recognizes that this is the sign. This is the moment. He or she at once takes the hint and sets off to bring matters to a head. We watch, realizing that, even though we didn't know such a sign was coming, we are now witnessing its effects.

Actually, those with eyes to see might have spotted that some such sign was imminent. When Jesus rode into Jerusalem on the donkey, he was acting out – and many of the onlookers must have realized he was acting out – the strange scene from Zechariah 9.9. John quotes that verse in 12.15. But the passage isn't just about a king coming to his people riding on a donkey. It is about this same king going on to establish his peaceful rule over the whole world, 'from sea to sea, and from the River to the ends of the earth'. The prophet is echoing many older passages, not least in the Psalms, which say substantially the same thing.

Thus, though Jesus has conducted his public career only among Jews (and of course Samaritans, as in John's famous chapter 4), there has always been the implication that if he was indeed Israel's Messiah the time would surely come when not only Israel but also the rest of the world would come to him. Not, we presume, in the sense of a normal earthly empire: Jesus wasn't being a standard 'king of the Jews', and there's no reason to suppose he was thinking of being a typical worldly emperor either! But John is already pointing us in the right direction when he says, in verse 19, that the Pharisees, sneering, declared that 'the world has gone off after him'. They mean, of course, 'look, all the riff-raff are dancing attendance on him'. But John sees deeper. It is indeed time for the world to come.

So when the Greeks send a message, via Philip and Andrew, to Jesus, what appears at first sight as a complete *non sequitur* (Jesus begins to talk about a grain of wheat falling into the earth and dying) is in fact the long prelude to his answer. We are not told whether the Greeks ever got to see Jesus, or what he said to them if they did. What John highlights is, for him, far more important. This is the moment for 'the son of man to be glorified' – for Jesus, in other words, to be 'lifted up', both on the cross and as the sign to the world, the sign that God's purpose for Israel is fulfilled and that now *it's time for the nations to come in.* 'When I've been lifted up from the earth, I will draw all people to myself' (verse 32).

And all this will happen because this is how God is glorifying his name and calling the whole world to account. The reason the non-Jewish world has not, up to this point, come to worship the creator God, the God of Israel, is that it has been under the control of the malign force to which Jesus here refers as 'this world's ruler'. He presumably means the satan, the adversary, the dark power that has usurped the creator's authority, the power that needs to be overthrown if God's kingdom is to come on earth as in heaven. And Jesus sees the request of the Greeks as the sign that all of this is about to kick into operation. He will be 'lifted up'; God will glorify his name; the seed will fall into the earth and die, and will by that means bear much fruit. Jesus' own challenge to his followers ('If you love your life, you'll lose it. If you hate your life in this world, you'll keep it for the life of the coming age', verse 25) is coming true in his own case, though it must also be acted out by his followers (verse 26). And, as a result, people from all across the world will be drawn to him.

111

And, whether the sceptics like it or not (they don't, of course), it has happened. Anyone looking on at the time would have waved it away as a grandiose dream. What can this mad young prophet be thinking of, to suppose that the death which he knew was already being planned for him would have any such effect? Yet, as we read this gospel this weekend, millions upon millions of our brother and sister Christians around the world, in places wondrously diverse and with worship styles more diverse again, hail him as 'Lord'.

It is, of course, our tragedy in the Western world that we have reduced the significance of that to 'private religion'. For most of the world it can never be that. Following Jesus as the true Lord means, for many today, precisely that: following him in risking his life (verse 26). But that, today as for Jesus, is the way God is glorified.

What are the hints, the secret signs, in today's world that indicate where God is doing a new work, and asking us to devote ourselves to taking it forwards?

Today

Lord Jesus Christ, lifted up on the cross, draw us and all the world to follow you, to serve you, and to glorify God.

WEEK 5: SUNDAY

Psalm 119.9–16

[9]How can young people keep their way pure?
　　By guarding it according to your word.
[10]With my whole heart I seek you;
　　do not let me stray from your commandments.
[11]I treasure your word in my heart,
　　so that I may not sin against you.
[12]Blessed are you, O LORD;
　　teach me your statutes.

¹³With my lips I declare
    all the ordinances of your mouth.
¹⁴ I delight in the way of your decrees
    as much as in all riches.
¹⁵I will meditate on your precepts,
    and fix my eyes on your ways.
¹⁶I will delight in your statutes;
    I will not forget your word.

'Sticks and stones may break my bones,' goes the old jingle, 'but words will never hurt me.' It's a lie. Don't believe it. Words are far, far more powerful than anything else. A sword can maim or kill, but only in the crudest of fashions, cutting off life as it was. A word can transform, for good or ill; it can build up a person's confidence or pull it down. When, some years ago, I was asked to reflect in public on the moments in my early life when people had helped me find my way, what came back to my mind, very strikingly, were half a dozen occasions when someone had said something, just a sentence or two, no great long lecture or anything – something that had opened up a new world that I knew I wanted to explore, a new pathway that I knew I had to walk. Those are the words that are worth their weight in gold, words that transformed my life far more thoroughly than any mere promises, bribes, threats or punishments could ever have done.

If that is true of human words – and often the people who speak those life-transforming words have no idea at the time of the long-term effect of what they're saying – how much more is it true of God's word. One of the great sorrows of our age is that people even inside the church, let alone outside it, have so reacted against the over-dogmatic claims of some 'conservative' Christians concerning the literal truth of the whole Bible (when a great deal is manifestly poetry, and so on), that the whole idea of the Bible itself as 'God's word' is discounted by many.

Here, as throughout Psalm 119, 'God's word' certainly refers to scripture – though of course it was the scriptures of the Old Testament, such as they were by the time the Psalm was written. And what we find here, a fitting meditation as we move into Passiontide, is an entire spirituality of a scripture-formed heart and mind. After all, we cannot understand Jesus himself, and his journey to the cross, except in terms of his being soaked in scripture, his own discovery in the Psalms and prophets of his unique vocation. We, following him however faintly, can do no better – though of course now with the full riches of both Testaments to call on.

This eight-verse stanza, the second in the long poem, divides into three parts. The first (verses 9–11) sees scripture as the key to protection against sin. The third (verses 14–16) celebrates God's word and God's law and announces a determination to make it more and more central to life. The two verses in the middle (verses 12–13) hold these (as it were) negative and positive emphases together, praising God publicly for his commandments.

The biblical vision of life includes, you see, the central component of the development of *character*. Far too often Christians have allowed themselves to think of their lives in terms of rules, a code of conduct to be kept (or, as it may be, broken). Rules appear external: they impinge on us from the outside. They appear to cramp our freedom, imposing someone else's ideas upon us. Many have reacted against a rule-based morality by thinking instead of the importance of 'being true to yourself', of being 'authentic' or 'spontaneous', 'doing what comes naturally'. Often the big debates in our churches about matters of behaviour are not in fact debates about the issues themselves but debates between people who believe in 'rules' and people who believe in 'authenticity'.

But the biblical vision works quite differently. God's word – whether the scriptures that the Psalmist knew or the scriptures that we have today – works on people the way words always work on people: by getting inside them and transforming them so that they see new possibilities, find ways of thinking about how they might be different, and gain courage to grow and change and make new, and previously impossible or unthinkable, decisions. 'Send forth your word, Lord,' goes the hymn, 'and let there be light.' The Psalmist would have agreed enthusiastically. When God's word does its work, we are not squashed into the wrong shape. We don't have our style cramped. We become more truly all that we were made to be, all that God wants us to be – because the word has done its work, has created new neural pathways in the brain, helped us make new connections. And enabled us to act on new convictions.

Those first three verses, then, are not simply 'negative' (some people are so allergic to any mention of 'sin' that one might almost suppose they had something to hide). We have to be sure, once more, that we are building on solid foundations. If we try to follow God while allowing impurity to fester (verse 9), while wandering off in various odd directions (verse 10) or simply while snapping our fingers in God's face and doing what we know he hates (verse 11), we won't get very far. God's word will help us at each one of those points, not by making it impossible for us to go off the rails but by opening our eyes to see what our actions and choices are really all about.

Then, as in verses 14–16, we will be able to build positively. We will start to take delight in scripture, discovering in it an inexhaustible mine of treasure. We will want to fix our eyes on it and not let our gaze wander. We will want to commit into the deepest recesses of our memory all that we are learning, so that it becomes part of us, in the way that what we eat and drink becomes part of us. This is how Christian character is formed.

Then, holding it all together, we will want to praise God (verse 12); and then, looking outwards, we will want to make public declaration of what his word is doing. Then we, too, will be contributing, in ways we cannot begin to imagine, to the same process in other people's lives. Our words, too, shaped and energized by God's words, will become part of God's work in guiding, warning, encouraging and building up God's people. A never-ending, outward-moving, spiral of grace. Jesus, on his way to the cross, stood at the heart of that spiral. The character that is formed by scripture is the character that follows him wherever he goes.

Today

Blessed are you, O Lord; teach me your statutes.

WEEK 5: MONDAY
Mark 11; focused on 11.12–25

[12]The next day, as they were leaving Bethany, Jesus was hungry. [13]From some distance away he saw a fig tree covered with leaves, and hoped to find some fruit on it; but when he came up to it he found nothing but leaves. (It wasn't yet the season for figs.)

[14]He addressed the tree directly. 'May no one ever eat fruit from you again,' he said. And his disciples heard.

[15]They came into Jerusalem. Jesus went into the Temple and began to drive out the traders, those who bought and sold in the Temple, and overturned the tables of the money-changers and the seats of the dove-sellers. [16]He permitted no one to carry any vessel through the Temple. [17]He began to teach: 'Isn't this what's written,' he said,

'My house shall be called
a house of prayer
for all the world to share?

But you've made it a brigands' den!'

[18]The chief priests and the legal experts heard, and looked for a way to get rid of him. But they were afraid of him, because the whole crowd was astonished at his teaching.

[19]When evening came, they went back out of the city.

²⁰As they were returning, early in the morning, they saw the fig tree withered from its roots.

²¹'Look, Teacher!' said Peter to Jesus, remembering what had happened before. 'The fig tree you cursed has withered.'

²²'Have faith in God,' replied Jesus. ²³'I'm telling you the truth: if anyone says to this mountain, "Be off with you – get yourself thrown into the sea", if they have no doubt in their heart, but believe that what they say will happen, it will be done for them. ²⁴That's why I'm telling you, everything that you request in prayer, everything you ask God for, believe that you receive it, and it will happen for you.

²⁵'And when you are standing there praying, if you have something against someone else, forgive them – so that your father in heaven may forgive you your trespasses.'

Imagine you are standing on a high hill, overlooking a long valley. In the valley are villages, a river, fields and woods, with a network of small roads winding their way between them all. Now imagine that you can see a car, driving much too fast, along one of those winding roads. The driver is obviously hell-bent on getting somewhere quicker than he should. At the same time, you see another car, coming the other way, going about its ordinary business. With horror, you see what's going to happen. Round one of the corners, any minute now . . .

Welcome to Mark 11. Jesus has been warning his fellow Jews, up and down the country, that God's kingdom is coming. But they, for the most part, have preferred their own aspirations, their own agendas. They have been speeding on their way, eager for national liberation of the usual revolutionary sort. Within the society, the rich have been getting richer, and the poor poorer. The self-appointed religious watchdogs have been concentrating on the outward rules and purity regulations rather than on the human heart. The Temple itself, the place where heaven and earth were supposed to meet, where God's forgiveness was supposed to happen, has been used as a symbol of national pride. They have ignored the warning signs

117

and are heading straight for a sharp bend ... where, coming the other way, is Jesus.

Jesus has been announcing that this was the time for God to become king. What's more, he had been making it happen – bringing God's fresh rule of healing and restoration to broken lives, families, households. He has been, in person, the place where heaven and earth meet, where forgiveness and all that goes with it have happened. And now he has come to Jerusalem, on a collision course with the Temple, granted what it has become. The place won't be big enough for both of them.

Mark, as we've seen elsewhere, writes the story almost like a novelist. He frames Jesus' action in the Temple (verses 15–18) within the double story of the fig tree. Jesus comes hoping for fruit, but finds none; so he puts a curse on the fig tree (verses 13–14). Then, the day after the Temple incident, there is the tree: withered from its roots (verses 20–21). The point could hardly be clearer. Jesus has come to Jerusalem, has come to the Temple, the holiest point in the Jewish world, looking for the fruit of repentance, of the wisdom, justice, holiness and peace that should be the marks of God's people. He has found none. His action in the Temple must be seen – certainly this is how Mark and the other gospel writers see it – as an acted parable of God's judgment. No one will eat fruit from this tree again.

That is why, by the way, all the stories that follow in the next two chapters reflect, in one way or another, the question of Jesus and the Temple. They lead the eye up to chapter 13, which is Jesus' main, final, prophetic warning against the Temple. And this long sequence, in turn, is Mark's deliberate build-up to the question of Jesus' death. If you want to understand why Jesus dies on the cross, you need to think long and hard about what it means that he was what the Temple had been, the place where heaven and earth met, the place of sacrifice and forgiveness.

At the heart of Jesus' charge against the Temple is the little verse from Isaiah 56.7. God's house was supposed, in the long run, to be a place of prayer for all the world. All the nations were supposed to look to Jerusalem and see it as a beacon of hope, of the presence of the creator God. Instead, anyone looking would see only a market-place, and worse: a den of brigands (an allusion to Jeremiah 7.11). 'Brigands' are more than 'robbers' (one of the traditional translations). 'Brigands' were, in Jesus' day, the holy revolutionaries, the terrorists, eager to overthrow pagan rule by violence. The Temple itself has come to symbolize that deep distortion of God's kingdom. The only word that can now be spoken to it is a word of judgment.

The disciples, watching in amazement, learn another lesson as well. They will be faced with 'this mountain' – the mountain where the Temple sits, ruled over by the hard-hearted chief priests – in the days to come. They will need to have faith that God will overthrow the system and all that it represents. The lesson goes wider, in line with Jesus' repeated teaching about prayer and faith. Ask; believe; and it will happen. But remember: while asking, forgive (verse 25). The door that opens to let forgiveness out of your heart towards someone else is the door through which God's forgiveness will enter.

As you look at today's world, where are the cars that are speeding much too fast towards the dangerous bends? Where are Jesus' warnings most badly needed in our world?

Today

Almighty Father, God of judgment and mercy, overthrow the systems that abuse their calling and oppress your people, and set up your rule of grace and peace.

WEEK 5: TUESDAY
Mark 12.1–17; focused on 12.1–12

¹Jesus began to speak to them with parables.

'Once upon a time,' he began, 'there was a man who planted a vineyard. He built a fence around it, dug out a wine-press, built a watchtower, and then let it out to tenant farmers. He himself went abroad. ²When the time came he sent a slave to the farmers to collect from them his portion of the vineyard's produce. ³They seized him, beat him and sent him away empty-handed.

⁴So again he sent another slave to them. This one they beat about the head, and treated shamefully. ⁵He sent another, and they killed him. He sent several more; they beat some and killed others.

⁶He had one more to send: his beloved son. He sent him to them last of all, thinking "They will respect my son".

⁷But the tenant farmers said to themselves,

"This is the heir! Come on – let's kill him, and we'll get the inheritance!" ⁸So they seized him and killed him, and threw him out of the vineyard.

⁹So what will the vineyard owner do? He will come and destroy those tenants, and give the vineyard to others. ¹⁰Or haven't you read the scripture which says,

There is the stone the builders refused;
now it's in place at the top of the corner.
¹¹This happened the way the Lord planned it;
we were astonished to see it.'

¹²They tried to find a way of arresting him, because they realized he had directed the parable against them. But they were afraid of the crowd. They left him and went away.

Mark Twain is reputed to have said that history never repeats itself, but that it often rhymes. In other words, although every event is unique, many events resemble others. They fall into a pattern. Sometimes, looking back along the line of unrepeatable events, one may detect a kind of poetry. A sequence that makes sense, that echoes and resonates down the years.

There are two senses in which the present passage, one of Jesus' most famous stories, 'rhymes' in that sort of way. To begin with, rather obviously within the story itself, the point

Jesus is making is that the vineyard owner has sent one servant after another to the vineyard, and each one has been treated – well, not exactly alike, but all alike with violence and contempt. This reaches a crescendo when the owner sends his own beloved son. This is how it works, Jesus is saying; listen for the rhyme, and see what's going to happen next.

Behind this story itself, at the level of Jesus' own ministry, we hear other echoes, other rhymes: of Jesus coming to look for figs on the fig tree and, finding none, pronouncing a solemn curse on the tree. It was, as we saw, a sign of his coming to Jerusalem looking for the fruit of obedience to God's way and his purposes, and, finding none, acting out dramatically God's judgment on the Temple itself. Now he tells a story of people coming to look for fruit, not from a fig tree but from a vineyard; and this time, instead of the plants being in trouble, it is the tenant farmers.

The second sense in which the present passage 'rhymes' is that Jesus is standing, and must have been conscious of standing, in a long line of prophets who have told similar stories, with similar intent. Chief among them is Isaiah, who in chapter 5 wrote a song about a vineyard – the vineyard which was Israel itself, the people who should have produced the fruit of justice and right living, but who instead produced only the wild grapes of wickedness and violence (Isaiah 5.7).

But there were other echoes, other 'rhymes', in the long Jewish tradition. Daniel interpreted the king's dream of a statue made of four metals being overthrown by a 'stone' which smashed it on its feet and which, in turn became a kingdom (Daniel 2). Jesus speaks, at the end of his story, of the 'stone' that the builders refused; and, in Hebrew, the word 'stone' and the word 'son' are very similar, as by coincidence they are in English too. Take away the 't' and the 'e' from 'stone', and you have 'son'. Take away the *e* from *eben*, 'stone', in Hebrew, and you have *ben*, 'son'. Here is the story, then, of the sequence of events leading up to the coming of the 'son'.

Remember where all this is taking place, and why, and yet another 'rhyme' emerges. Jesus is still explaining why he has done what he has done in the Temple. The Temple will be destroyed, but his kingdom-work will go on and be vindicated by events. This time the echo is of Psalm 118.22–23, which speaks of a 'stone', lying perhaps in the builders' yard, but of the wrong shape to fit anywhere in the wall. Only when the builders get to the very top, and look around for a stone which will do to finish off the top corner, will they realize that the stone they have ignored up to that point is the very one they now need. In the same way, Jesus is saying, he has come to Jerusalem with the message of God's kingdom, but this message simply won't fit into the 'building' of Judaism the way the present builders (the chief priests, Herod, the Pharisees) have been constructing it. They will realize too late that he belongs at the very top of the true building. But by then the vineyard owner will have come to 'destroy those tenants, and give the vineyard to others' (verse 9).

This story is as shocking today as it was to Jesus' first hearers. That can't be avoided. We are on a Lenten journey, after all, which we know will end at the foot of the cross; and the cross, as Paul said, is foolishness to pagans and a scandal to Jews. All those other sayings about selling everything to buy the one great pearl, or giving everything you've got to get the field with the buried treasure, come to mind. The story, in other words, 'rhymes' with so much else in Jesus' teaching.

But what does it rhyme with in our own lives? Has God been sending one message after another to us, corporately or individually, which we've been steadfastly ignoring? Which prophetic words has our proud modern culture refused to hear, pouring scorn on the messengers and making fun of those who listen to them? Which voices have you done your best not to hear? Listen for the rhymes. When push comes to shove, are we going to celebrate Jesus' enthronement at the top of the new 'Temple', or are we going to treat him as simply a misshapen piece of stone for which we can see no purpose?

Today

Come to us, King Jesus, with your word of warning, and give us ears to hear and hearts to enthrone you as Lord.

WEEK 5: WEDNESDAY
Mark 12.18–44; focused on 12.18–27

[18]Some Sadducees approached Jesus (Sadducees, by the way, deny the resurrection).

[19]'Teacher,' they said, 'Moses wrote for us that "If a man's brother dies, and leaves a wife but no child, the brother should take the wife and raise up descendants for his brother." [20]Well now: there were once seven brothers. The first married a wife, and died without children. [21]The second married the widow, and died without children. The third did so as well, [22]and so did all seven, still without leaving children. Finally the woman died too. [23]So: when they rise again in the resurrection, whose wife will she be? All seven had her, after all.'

[24]'Where you're going wrong', replied Jesus, 'is that you don't know the scriptures, or God's power. [25]When people rise from the dead, they don't marry, nor do people give them in marriage. They are like angels in heaven.

[26]'However, to show that the dead are indeed to be raised, surely you've read in the book of Moses, in the passage about the bush, what God says to Moses? "I am Abraham's God, Isaac's God and Jacob's God"? [27]He isn't the God of the dead, but of the living. You are completely mistaken.'

James stared at the machine doubtfully. 'I don't know,' he said. 'Looks quite clever, but I can't see how it can ever actually work.'

His brother, who had spent all winter building the new machine – they were farmers, and needed a better way of harvesting their crop – turned to him with a smile. 'You're forgetting one thing,' he said. 'The new fuel they're producing. It's much lighter than diesel or petrol. Yes, it would never work with the old stuff. But you just wait. With the new fuel, it'll do everything we need and more.'

The missing ingredient. Actually, in Jesus' debate with the Sadducees there were two missing ingredients. In addition to the power – God's power, which they had conveniently left out of the equation – there were the scriptures.

But didn't the Sadducees know the scriptures? Weren't they the official guardians of the whole ancestral tradition, the aristocracy who were supposed to be looking after the very heart of Judaism? How come they were – from Jesus' point of view – so far off beam?

To answer this will also answer the question that some might ask: why does this odd little story appear at this point in the first place? Mark 11 and 12 are not just a collection of debates that Jesus happened to have in his final days in Jerusalem. They all relate, in one way or another, to the question of the kingdom: just what was going to happen when God became king, and how would this relate to the world they were living in at the time?

Here's the clue. The Sadducees were the powerful elite in Jerusalem. Like most elite groups, they hugged power close to themselves, and were deeply suspicious of any radical movements that suggested that things were going to be changed, turned upside down. That's why they opposed the teaching of the resurrection, which was very popular with the Pharisees: because 'resurrection', God bringing dead people back to life again to people his new world, meant a root-and-branch transformation of the whole world. There was no guarantee that those presently in power would retain that power in the new world. In fact, as Jesus had been saying frequently, there was every likelihood that those in the front would end up at the back, and vice versa. If people start believing that sort of thing, the Sadducees reckoned, there was no knowing what they might go and do.

So the Sadducees did what people today will do when they want to rubbish an idea they are frightened of. Tell silly stories to show how ridiculous it is. (That went on, by the way, into the time of the early church. The great second-century teacher Tertullian tells of people who, sneeringly, ask what would happen if a cannibal eats a Christian and then the cannibal himself converts and becomes a Christian. At the resurrection, who will have which bits of body?) So the Sadducees produce their story about the woman with seven husbands. At the resurrection, whose wife will she be?

They have forgotten the missing ingredient: the scriptures and the power of God. The whole point of the resurrection, Jesus insists, is that it isn't just a coming back into the present life, with its marrying and childbearing. In God's new world, those who rise from the dead will be, in this respect (but only in this respect), like the angels: they won't need to marry, because there will be no more death, and no need for more children. (That doesn't mean, in case you were wondering, that there will be no more joyful and intimate human relationships. The greatest of our present human delights is a mere signpost to the far greater, presently unimaginable, joys of living in God's new world.) God is the creator; he is not limited by the possibilities of the present, corruptible world.

This, too, is taught in the scriptures, if you know where to look. The Sadducees, deeply conservative as they were, were suspicious of all the 'later' books of the Bible, and concentrated only on the first five. Very well, says Jesus, let's go there. What do we find? We find God declaring to Moses that he is the God of Abraham, Isaac and Jacob – and we know he is the God of the living, not of the dead.

What does this mean? That Abraham, Isaac and Jacob have already been raised from the dead? Certainly not. 'Resurrection' never meant 'going to heaven' or 'living on in the presence of

God'. It meant new bodies. But if people were going to be given new bodies, that meant that between their death and their eventual resurrection they were still, in fact, alive in some sense in the presence of God. Jesus, like the Pharisees in this respect, taught *a two-stage 'life after death'*: first, a time of being 'with God', alive in his presence but not yet re-embodied, and then, after that, the newly embodied life of resurrection itself.

This is a stunning piece of teaching, as the legal expert who now approached Jesus (verse 28) realized. It not only reaffirms the great truth that God has prepared for his people a far more glorious future than most of them ever imagine. It also strongly reaffirms the rightness of what Jesus was doing in the Temple. God was launching, through Jesus, his sovereign, saving rule, and everything was indeed going to be turned upside down by it. The Sadducees' power base – the Temple – was going to be overthrown, and God was going to set up Jesus himself, and his followers, as the new, radical alternative. This would be a bit like 'resurrection' in advance: God's new life, on earth as in heaven.

Sounds a bit dubious? You're forgetting the missing ingredients: the scriptures and the power of God.

Today

Give us faith, heavenly Father, to believe in your power, and to celebrate your world-changing promises.

WEEK 5: THURSDAY

Mark 13; focused on 13.1–23

[1]As they were going out of the Temple, one of Jesus' disciples said to him, 'Teacher! Look at these huge stones, and these huge buildings!'

[2]'You see these enormous buildings?' said Jesus. 'There will not be one single stone left on top of another. They will all be torn down.'

³Peter, James, John and Andrew approached him privately as he was sitting on the Mount of Olives opposite the Temple.

⁴'Tell us,' they asked. 'When will these things happen? What will be the sign that these things are about to be completed?'

⁵'Take care that nobody deceives you,' Jesus began to say to them. ⁶'Plenty of people will come in my name, saying "I'm the one!", and they will lead plenty astray. ⁷But whenever you hear about wars, and rumours about wars, don't be disturbed. These things have to happen, but it doesn't mean the end is here. ⁸One nation will rise up against another; one kingdom will rise up against another. There will be earthquakes from place to place, and famines too. These are the first pains of childbirth.

⁹'But watch out for yourselves. They will hand you over to courts, they will beat you in synagogues; you will stand before rulers and kings because of me, as a witness against them. ¹⁰And the message of the kingdom must first be announced to all the nations. ¹¹And when they put you on trial and hand you over, don't work out beforehand what you are going to say, but say whatever is given you at that moment. It won't be you speaking, you see, but the holy spirit.

¹²'One brother will hand over another to death. Fathers will hand over children. Children will rebel against parents and have them put to death. ¹³And you will be hated by everyone because of my name. But the one who is patient through to the end – that one will be saved.

¹⁴'However,' Jesus continued, 'when you see "the desolating abomination" set up where it ought not to be' (let the reader understand) 'then those who are in Judaea should run away to the mountains. ¹⁵If you're on the housetop, don't go down, and don't go in to get anything from the house. ¹⁶If you're out in the countryside, don't turn back again to pick up your cloak.

¹⁷'It will be a terrible time for pregnant and nursing mothers. ¹⁸Pray that it won't happen in winter. ¹⁹Yes, those days will bring trouble like nothing that's ever happened from the beginning of creation, which God created, until now, or ever will again. ²⁰In fact, if the Lord had not shortened the

days, no one would be rescued. But for the sake of his chosen ones, those whom he appointed, he shortened the days.

[21]'So at that time, if someone says to you, "Look – here is the Messiah!" or, "Look – there he is!", don't believe them; [22]because false messiahs and false prophets will arise, and will perform signs and portents to lead astray even God's chosen ones, if that were possible. [23]But you must be on your guard. I've told you everything ahead of time.'

I have inherited from my father a splendid old set of nineteenth-century books. (Yes, I had quite a lot of books already, but there is always room for a few more.) This particular set is a collection of writing, and drawing, from the old humorous magazine called *Punch*, which ran for well over a century from its inception in 1841 before folding, sadly, in 1992. (It was revived in 1996, but collapsed again in 2002.) The books reflect the early part of that time.

Many of the articles are period pieces, still witty and worth reading both in themselves and as a document, now, of social history. Many of the cartoons, too, have retained their quirky humour. Indeed, it was *Punch* that helped to popularize the modern meaning of the word 'cartoon' as a humorous drawing or illustration. Before then, the word had simply referred to a preliminary sketch that an artist or architect might make before producing the finished product.

But some of the cartoons are completely opaque to me now. They depend entirely for their point on a shared set of symbols: on particular animals representing particular politicians, and so on (much as, today, donkeys and elephants represent America's two main political parties). And the trouble with that, of course, is that if you don't know the key – if you don't know which figures represent what, or indeed who the key politicians of the day were, and what were the major issues that they confronted – then you simply won't get the point. You might even suppose, seeing a picture with a zebra, a tortoise and an ostrich deep in conversation, that the artist was producing a fantasy about life in a zoo.

With an old cartoon we don't understand, we smile, shake our heads, and turn to something more accessible. But when the same thing happens in the Bible, we often fail to realize what sort of document we are reading, and suppose that the writer intends every word to be taken in a kind of flat, literal fashion.

That has been the fate, in particular, of this chapter, Mark 13, and others like it. Many have looked ahead to verses 24–27, and have noted the prediction of the sun and the moon being darkened and the stars falling from heaven, together with 'the son of man coming on clouds with great power and glory'. Ah, they think, this must be the end of the world! This is the collapse of the cosmos! Creation is going to implode, Jesus will return, and the world will cease to be!

And Mark would look on, like a nineteenth-century cartoon-ist shaking his head at an incomprehending twenty-first-century reader, and say, 'No: that's not how the language works. You don't know the Bible, or the power of God.' The sun, the moon and the stars are regularly used in the Bible as code for 'the powers of the world' – meaning, in our day, the *political* powers; and the passage quoted in verses 24 and 25 in fact comes from Isaiah's description of the fall of Babylon (Isaiah 13.10). The 'coming of the son of man', as in verse 26, we shall deal with next week.

In fact, verses 1–23, the passage on which we focus here, make it quite clear that what Jesus is warning about is the fall of Jerusalem, and the terrifying events that will lead up to it. That's where the passage starts, with Jesus prophesying quite explicitly the destruction of the Temple, and the disciples then asking him about it: when will it happen, and how will they know (verse 4)? We should assume, granted this beginning, that the rest of the passage will constitute an answer, or a set of answers, to this question.

The answer comes in three main stages. First (verses 5–8), there will be a time of turmoil: plenty of worrying things happening (wars, earthquakes and so on), but these will not be the key signs. Second (verses 9–13), this will be a time when Jesus' followers are isolated, persecuted, misunderstood and quite possibly killed. At times of great political tension, people who refuse to join in with the currently fashionable mood will be hated by everyone else. So this is a call for patience.

But, third, there will be a particular sign (verses 14–23). Look at the prophet Daniel. In Daniel 9.37 he speaks of an 'abomination that desolates', something horrible and scandalous that, by its very presence, causes the place to be like a wilderness. This is picked up in Daniel 11.31 and 12.11. What could this be?

Two centuries before the time of Jesus, and still vivid in folk memory, the Syrian tyrant Antiochus Epiphanes had turned the Jerusalem Temple into a pagan shrine. Well, something like that would happen again. Perhaps it would be an emperor putting up a huge statue of himself and demanding (as in Daniel 2) that people worship it. That almost happened in AD 40, when the mad Roman emperor Gaius Caligula tried to force such a thing upon Jerusalem. (The plan was halted when he was assassinated in January 41.)

But something like it would happen again; of that there could be no doubt. Anyone living in Jerusalem when the Romans finally closed in in AD 68–69, before the Temple's destruction in 70, would be able to see the signs: Roman standards being planted in the sacred precincts themselves. That would be the moment, declared Jesus, when you should get out and run (verses 14–20). That makes no sense if Mark thought Jesus was talking about the end of the world. It makes every sense if you're faced with an imminent enemy siege. And when that happens (verses 21–23), don't be fooled: there will be plenty of would-be 'messiahs' showing up, but they must stay loyal to Jesus.

Today

Give us courage and faith, good Lord, to hold on to you and your word when all around us seems to be shaking and turbulent.

WEEK 5: FRIDAY
Mark 11.1–11

[1]So they approached Jerusalem. They got as far as Bethphage and Bethany, on the Mount of Olives, when Jesus sent two of his disciples on ahead with a specific task.

[2]'Go to the village over there,' he said to them, 'and as soon as you enter it you will find a colt tied up – one that nobody has ever ridden before. Untie it and bring it here. [3]And if anyone says to you, "Why are you doing that?" then say, "The master needs it, and he will return it at once."'

[4]They went off and found the colt tied up beside a door, out in the street; and they untied it.

[5]Some of the bystanders said to them, 'Why are you untying the colt?' [6]They gave the answer Jesus had told them, and they let them carry on. [7]So they brought the colt to Jesus and laid their cloaks on it, and he mounted it. [8]Several people spread their cloaks out in the road. Others did the same with foliage that they had cut in the fields. [9]Those in front, and those coming behind, shouted out, 'Hosanna! Welcome in the Lord's Name! [10]Welcome to the kingdom of our father David, the kingdom coming right now! Hosanna in the highest!'

[11]Jesus entered Jerusalem, went into the Temple, and looked all round. It was already getting late, and he returned to Bethany with the Twelve.

It was late October 1991. The fishing boat *Andrea Gail* was five hundred miles out into the Atlantic, off the Massachusetts coast. A cold front was moving along the US–Canada border, causing turbulent weather in New England, while at the same time a high-pressure system was building over south-eastern Canada. These two systems would, without extra help, have created quite a storm; but there was more. A tropical hurricane, arriving from further south, completed the picture. It was the perfect storm. Ferocious winds and huge waves reduced the *Andrea Gail* boat to matchwood. There had, of course, been earlier 'perfect storms', but this was the one made famous by a book and a movie which took that phrase as their title.

I have often thought that when Jesus rode into Jerusalem on that first Palm Sunday, for which we are now getting ready as our Lenten journey nears its end, he was riding into a perfect storm. The strong wind from the west is the pressure from the Roman empire: Rome needed the Middle East to be stable and settled to keep its eastern frontier secure. The high-pressure system to the north is the eager, overheated aspirations of the Jewish people, longing for independence and ready to use violence to achieve it. And the hurricane from the south? The hurricane from the south is the ancient, long-prophesied purpose of God himself.

The Jews, of course, hoped that God would simply endorse their aspirations. Get the hurricane to reinforce the high-pressure system, and we can see off the cold westerly wind! But throughout the long history of Israel things had never been that simple. Again and again God's purposes went ahead while Israel misunderstood them, misread the signals, and tried to pull God's plan out of shape to coincide a bit more with its own dreams and goals. Sometimes this had resulted in major disasters.

What Jesus did, on that first Palm Sunday, was to put into action one of the classic statements of prophetic purpose. God would indeed come back to his people, to fulfil his promises, to rescue them, and to set up his kingdom of peace over the world. But it wouldn't happen the way they wanted. It would indeed be a kingdom to confront Rome and every other proud pagan empire. But it would also have to confront the twisted hopes and desires of the people themselves, not least their corrupt and self-serving leaders.

So, on Palm Sunday, Jesus rides, knowingly and deliberately, into the perfect storm. He knows what will happen. But he believes, as we shall see, that the storm now brewing will be, paradoxically, the means by which God's purposes will be accomplished.

All this explains the contrast, to which people often draw attention, between the enthusiasm of the crowds on Palm Sunday and the angry cries from the same crowd on Good Friday (15.10–15). And here Mark has to allow the words to carry two quite different meanings. When the crowd shouts out its Hosannas (verses 9–10), welcoming Jesus into the city, and celebrating 'the kingdom of our father David, the kingdom coming right now', they are thinking back a thousand years to the time when Israel was truly great, when the surrounding nations were repelled, and the independent kingdom of David, and then of his son Solomon, extended further than ever before or since. That's what they want. Like James and John in chapter 10, they are imagining Jesus as a standard earthly king – well, not exactly standard, because they certainly don't want him to be a Herod or a Caesar, but they certainly imagine that he will do what a true king should, get rid of the hated pagan oppressor and establish an independent country once and for all.

Mark, of course, believes firmly that Jesus is indeed the 'son of David', the one who is bringing God's kingdom on earth as in heaven. But that kingdom is not the sort the crowd have in mind, just as it wasn't the sort that James and John had in mind. Mark is beginning a sequence which will take us all the way to the foot of the cross, where people – here the crowds, there a Roman centurion, with others in between – will say things which they mean in one sense and which Mark 'hears', and wants us to hear, in quite another sense. Jesus is indeed to be crowned as the king of the Jews. But the crown will be the crown of thorns. And the homage that the nations will pay him at his coronation will be the muttered, head-shaking puzzlement of a hard-bitten professional killer.

Among the many other lessons we urgently need to learn from Palm Sunday is the way in which those perfect storms have a habit of coming back and catching us unawares. The world is trying to squeeze us into one particular mould. We may, particularly if we are Christians, have a fairly clear idea of what we want to do, how God wants us to be; but, as with the Jewish people of the first century, as indeed with James and John, there is often far too much of our own agenda peeping through. We need to learn humility: humility to realize that God's plans may well not be our plans, because his thoughts and ours may be just as radically different as God's thoughts were from the thoughts even of Jesus' closest disciples. Sometimes the only way we learn all this is through the perfect storm, the moment when everything in life appears to go wrong and we find ourselves tossed to and fro in the middle of it. When that happens, the answer we get from Palm Sunday is clear. Hold on. See the story through. Keep with Jesus in all that lies ahead. The story does indeed lead to the cross. But that is the moment, in a way that still catches us off guard, at which God's purposes are fulfilled, and his kingdom is established.

Today

Teach us, gracious Lord, to watch humbly for your way forward, no matter what our culture may say or our hearts may desire.

WEEK 5: SATURDAY

Mark 14.1—15.47

[1]Passover – the feast of unleavened bread – was due in two days. The chief priests and the lawyers were plotting how to seize Jesus by a trick, and kill him.

²'We can't do it at the feast,' they said. 'The people might riot.'

³Jesus was in Bethany, at the house of Simon (known as 'the Leper'). While he was at table, a woman came up with an alabaster pot containing extremely valuable ointment made of pure spikenard. She broke the pot and poured the ointment on Jesus' head.

⁴Some of the people there grumbled to one another.

'What's the point of wasting the ointment?' they asked. ⁵'That ointment could have been sold for three hundred dinars, and given to the poor.'

And they were angry with her.

⁶'Leave her alone,' said Jesus. 'Why make trouble for her? She has done a wonderful thing for me. ⁷You have the poor with you always; you can help them whenever you want to. But you won't always have me.

⁸'She has played her part. She has anointed my body for its burial, ahead of time. ⁹I'm telling you the truth: wherever the message is announced in all the world, the story of what she has just done will be told. That will be her memorial.'

¹⁰Judas Iscariot, one of the Twelve, went to the chief priests, to arrange to hand Jesus over to them. ¹¹They were delighted with his proposal, and made an agreement to pay him. And he began to look for a good moment to hand him over.

¹²On the first day of unleavened bread, when the Passover lambs were sacrificed, Jesus' disciples said to him, 'Where would you like us to go and get things ready for you to eat the Passover?'

¹³He sent off two of his disciples, with these instructions.

'Go into the city, and you will be met by a man carrying a water-pot. Follow him. ¹⁴When he goes indoors, say to the master of the house, "The teacher says, where is the guest room for me, where I can eat the Passover with my disciples?" ¹⁵He will show you a large upstairs room, set out and ready. Make preparations for us there.'

¹⁶The disciples went out, entered the city, and found it exactly as he had said. They prepared the Passover.

¹⁷When it was evening, Jesus came with the Twelve. ¹⁸As they were reclining at table and eating, Jesus said, 'I'm telling you the truth: one of you is going to betray me – one of you that's eating with me.'

¹⁹They began to be very upset, and they said to him, one after another, 'It isn't me, is it?'

²⁰'It's one of the Twelve,' said Jesus, 'one who has dipped his bread in the dish with me. ²¹Yes: the son of man is completing his journey, as scripture said he would; but it's bad news for the man who betrays him! It would have been better for that man never to have been born.'

²²While they were eating, he took bread, blessed it, broke it, and gave it to them.

'Take it,' he said. 'This is my body.'

²³Then he took the cup, gave thanks, and gave it to them, and they all drank from it.

²⁴'This is my blood of the covenant,' he said, 'which is poured out for many. ²⁵I'm telling you the truth: I won't ever drink from the fruit of the vine again, until that day – the day when I drink it new in the kingdom of God.'

²⁶They sang a hymn, and went out to the Mount of Olives.

²⁷'You're all going to desert me,' said Jesus, 'because it's written,

I shall attack the shepherd
and then the sheep will scatter.

²⁸'But after I am raised up, I will go ahead of you to Galilee.'

²⁹Peter spoke up.

'Everyone else may desert you,' he said, 'but I won't.'

³⁰'I'm telling you the truth,' Jesus replied. 'Today – this very night, before the cock has crowed twice – you will renounce me three times.'

³¹This made Peter all the more vehement.

'Even if I have to die with you,' he said, 'I will never renounce you.'

And all the rest said the same.

³²They came to a place called Gethsemane.

'Stay here', said Jesus to the disciples, 'while I pray.'

[33]He took Peter, James and John with him, and became quite overcome and deeply distressed.

[34]"My soul is disturbed within me", he said, 'right to the point of death. Stay here and keep watch.'

[35]He went a little further, and fell on the ground and prayed that, if possible, the moment might pass from him.

[36]'Abba, father,' he said, 'all things are possible for you! Take this cup away from me! But – not what I want, but what you want.'

[37]He returned and found them sleeping.

'Are you asleep, Simon?' he said to Peter. 'Couldn't you keep watch for a single hour? [38]Watch and pray, so that you won't come into the time of trouble. The spirit is eager, but the body is weak.'

[39]Once more he went off and prayed, saying the same words. [40]And again, when he returned, he found them asleep, because their eyes were very heavy. They had no words to answer him. [41]But the third time he came, he said to them, 'All right – sleep as much as you like now. Have a good rest. The job is done, the time has come – and look! The son of man is betrayed into the clutches of sinners. [42]Get up, let's be on our way. Here comes the man who's going to betray me.'

[43]At once, while he was still speaking, Judas, one of the Twelve, arrived, accompanied by a crowd, with swords and clubs, from the chief priests, the legal experts, and the elders. [44]The betrayer had given them a coded sign: 'The one I kiss – that's him! Seize him and take him away safely.'

[45]He came up to Jesus at once. 'Rabbi!' he said, and kissed him.

[46]The crowd laid hands on him and seized him. [47]One of the bystanders drew a sword and struck the high priest's servant, cutting off his ear. [48]Then Jesus spoke to them.

'Anyone would think', he said, 'you'd come after a brigand! Fancy needing swords and clubs to arrest me! [49]Day after day I've been teaching in the Temple, under your noses, and you never laid a finger on me. But the scriptures must be fulfilled.'

⁵⁰Then they all abandoned him and ran away.

⁵¹A young man had followed him, wearing only a linen tunic over his otherwise naked body. ⁵²They seized him, and he left the tunic and ran away naked.

⁵³They took Jesus away to the high priest. All the chief priests and the elders and legal experts were assembled. ⁵⁴Peter followed him at a distance, and came to the courtyard of the high priest's house, where he sat with the servants and warmed himself at the fire.

⁵⁵The chief priests, and all the Sanhedrin, looked for evidence for a capital charge against Jesus, but they didn't find any. ⁵⁶Several people invented fictitious charges against him, but their evidence didn't agree. ⁵⁷Then some stood up with this fabricated charge: ⁵⁸'We heard him say, "I will destroy this Temple, which human hands have made, and in three days I'll build another, made without human hands."'

⁵⁹But even so their evidence didn't agree.

⁶⁰Then the high priest got up in front of them all and interrogated Jesus.

'Haven't you got any answer about whatever it is these people are testifying against you?'

⁶¹Jesus remained silent, and didn't answer a word.

Once more the high priest questioned him.

'Are you the Messiah, the Son of the Blessed One?'

⁶²'I am,' replied Jesus, 'and you will see "the son of man sitting at the right hand of Power, and coming with the clouds of heaven".'

⁶³'Why do we need any more evidence?' shouted the high priest, tearing his clothes. ⁶⁴'You heard the blasphemy! What's your verdict?'

They all agreed on their judgment: he deserved to die.

⁶⁵Some of them began to spit at him. They blindfolded him and hit him, and said, 'Prophesy!' And the servants took charge of him and beat him.

⁶⁶Peter, meanwhile, was below in the courtyard. One of the high priest's servant-girls came up ⁶⁷and saw him warming himself. She looked closely at him, and said, 'You were with Jesus the Nazarene too, weren't you?'

⁶⁸'I don't know what on earth you're talking about,' replied Peter.

He went outside into the forecourt, and the cock crowed.

⁶⁹The servant-girl saw him, and once more began to say to the bystanders, 'This man is one of them.' ⁷⁰But Peter again denied it.

A little while later the bystanders said again to Peter, 'You really are one of them, aren't you? You're a Galilean!'

⁷¹At that he began to curse and swear, 'I don't know this man you're talking about.' ⁷²And immediately the cock crowed for the second time. Then Peter remembered the words that Jesus had said to him: 'Before the cock crows twice, you will renounce me three times.' And he burst into tears.

15 ¹As soon as morning came, the chief priests held a council meeting with the elders, the legal experts, and the whole Sanhedrin. They bound Jesus, took him off to Pilate, and handed him over.

²'Are you the king of the Jews?' asked Pilate.

'You have said it,' replied Jesus.

³The chief priests laid many accusations against him.

⁴Pilate again interrogated him: 'Aren't you going to make any reply? Look how many things they're accusing you of!'

⁵But Jesus gave no reply at all, which astonished Pilate.

⁶The custom was that at festival time he used to release for them a single prisoner, whoever they would ask for. ⁷There was a man in prison named Barabbas, one of the revolutionaries who had committed murder during the uprising. ⁸So the crowd came up and began to ask Pilate to do what he normally did.

⁹'Do you want me', answered Pilate, 'to release for you "the king of the Jews"?'

¹⁰He said this because he knew that the chief priests had handed him over out of envy. ¹¹The chief priests stirred up the crowd to ask for Barabbas instead to be released to them. So Pilate once again asked them, ¹²'What then do you want me to do with the one you call "the king of the Jews"?'

¹³'Crucify him!' they shouted again.

¹⁴'Why?' asked Pilate. 'What has he done wrong?'

'Crucify him!' they shouted all the louder.

[15]Pilate wanted to satisfy the crowd; so he released Barabbas for them. He had Jesus flogged, and handed him over to be crucified.

[16]The soldiers took Jesus into the courtyard, that is, the Praetorium, and called together the whole squad. [17]They dressed Jesus up in purple; then, weaving together a crown of thorns, they stuck it on him. [18]They began to salute him: 'Greetings, King of the Jews!' [19]And they hit him over the head with a staff, and spat at him, and knelt down to do him homage. [20]Then, when they had mocked him, they took the purple robe off him, and put his own clothes back on.

Then they led him off to crucify him. [21]They compelled a man called Simon to carry Jesus' cross. He was from Cyrene, and was coming in from out of town. He was the father of Alexander and Rufus.

[22]They took Jesus to the place called Golgotha, which in translation means 'Skull's Place'. [23]They gave him a mixture of wine and myrrh, but he didn't drink it.

[24]So they crucified him; they 'parted his clothing between them, casting lots' to see who would get what. [25]It was about nine o'clock in the morning when they crucified him. [26]The inscription, giving the charge, read: 'The King of the Jews'. [27]They also crucified two bandits alongside him, one on his right and one on his left.

[29]People who were passing by abused him. They shook their heads at him.

'Hah!' they said. 'You were going to destroy the Temple, were you? And build it again in three days? [30]Why don't you rescue yourself, and come down from the cross?'

[31]The chief priests and the lawyers were mocking him in the same way among themselves.

'He rescued others,' they said, 'but he can't rescue himself. [32]Messiah, is he? King of Israel, did he say? Well, let's see him come down from the cross! We'll believe him when we see that!'

The two who were crucified alongside him taunted him as well.

140

³³At midday there was darkness over all the land until three in the afternoon. ³⁴At three o'clock Jesus shouted out in a powerful voice, '*Eloi, Eloi, lema sabachthani?*' which means, 'My God, my God, why did you abandon me?'

³⁵When the bystanders heard it, some of them said, 'He's calling for Elijah!'

³⁶One of them ran and filled a sponge with sour wine, put it on a pole, and gave it him to drink.

'Well then,' he declared, 'let's see if Elijah will come and take him down.'

³⁷But Jesus, with another loud shout, breathed his last.

³⁸The Temple veil was torn in two, from top to bottom. ³⁹When the centurion who was standing facing him saw that he died in this way, he said, 'This fellow really was God's son.'

⁴⁰Some women were watching from a distance. They included Mary Magdalene, Mary the mother of the younger James and of Joses, and Salome. ⁴¹They had followed Jesus in Galilee, and had attended to his needs. There were several other women, too, who had come up with him to Jerusalem.

⁴²It was already getting towards evening, and it was the day of Preparation, that is, the day before the sabbath. ⁴³Joseph of Arimathea, a reputable member of the Council who was himself eagerly awaiting God's kingdom, took his courage in both hands, went to Pilate, and requested the body of Jesus.

⁴⁴Pilate was surprised that he was already dead. He summoned the centurion, and asked whether he had been dead for some time. ⁴⁵When he learned the facts from the centurion, he conceded the body to Joseph.

⁴⁶So Joseph bought a linen cloth, took the body down, wrapped it in the cloth, and laid it in a tomb cut out of the rock. He rolled a stone against the door of the tomb. ⁴⁷Mary Magdalene and Mary the mother of Joses saw where he was buried.

Reports suggest that there are plenty of people today who are so distant from the story of Jesus that they can watch a children's play about him without realizing what's going to happen. They are then shocked to the core at the thought of the terrible events that unfold so swiftly. How could they do that, such people think, to someone like Jesus?

Part of the challenge of this weekend, as we prepare for the week that changed the world for ever, is that we need to be, once again, shockable by this story. How easy it is for regular churchgoers, and even those who used to be regular but are no more, to go through Mark chapters 14 and 15 and mentally tick off the different incidents. Oh yes, there's that bit. Oh yes, Jesus before the chief priests. And then Pontius Pilate. And so Jesus goes to be . . .

And we ought to be saying to ourselves: 'Crucified? That's crazy! You can't do that!' We ought to want to jump up from our chairs and rush to the rescue. How can they even think of sending Jesus to his death? In most countries in the Western world, capital punishment has long been abolished, and when those of us who take that for granted then hear of people being executed in cold blood, whether in Iran or in Texas, we are horrified, and want to write to the newspapers, or to our members of Parliament, to anyone, in protest. But we ought to have that same reaction magnified a million times as we read the story of Jesus' death. This was one of the cruellest things ever done, one of the most unjust things ever done, one of the wickedest things ever done.

It was also the moment when God did the most loving thing of all; the moment when God unveiled his justice once and for all; the moment when God's mercy overflowed, through the one man Jesus, for all. How can this be? How can we hold on in our hearts and minds to these two utterly different readings of the same event?

The easy answers are there, and they are all true. He died to save us. He died for our sins. He died because 'he loved us and gave himself for us'. Yes. Cling on to those. We need them.

But there is more, much more. The easy and well-known answers are signposts to a larger reality, less easy to capture in slogans. Some of the greatest truths in life can't be caught in the butterfly net of a phrase here, a neat little dogma there. If you try, you will end up simply pinning them to the page; the butterfly is beautiful, but it will be dead. What we need to do instead is to let the creature fly, let it spread its wings and do what it does best, while we look on in wonder. And that is the task to which Mark invites us now.

His explanation of the reasons why Jesus died draw on everything that has gone before in his story. The story he tells is the climax of the story of Israel itself; and the story of Jesus' death is the climax of the climax, the point where God's age-old purpose for Israel is finally unveiled. Mark has hinted at this, from Jesus' baptism onwards. The scriptures pointed to it, whether the passages that spoke of Jesus as God's son, to be enthroned as the true king, or the passages that spoke of him as the servant, come to inaugurate God's kingdom by dying a shameful death. All that is important, but it will simply get us to the starting point.

The starting point, as we find it in the first verse of chapter 14, is the festival and the plot.

The festival! Passover, of course. The time when God went down to Egypt to rescue his people from their slavery. Jesus has chosen this moment, when everyone is coming to Jerusalem, everyone is telling the story of God's great rescue operation, God's covenant with his people, God's revelation of his name and his character in overthrowing the pagan enemy (in that case, Egypt, but most people had no difficulty in translating 'Egypt' into 'Rome') and bringing his people out into freedom. Jesus chose this moment because (Mark is telling us) he believed it was time for the ultimate Passover, the Passover of Passovers. God had come back in person and was revealing himself and his powerful love in a way never before imagined but never again to be doubted.

And the plot. All through Mark's gospel we have seen the plots being considered, and sometimes attempted. We have seen trick questions, mutterings behind hands, and, darkly, the accusations. He's in league with the devil. He's breaking the sabbath. He's blaspheming – who does he think he is to be forgiving sins? He's leading the people astray. And now the sequence begins: why this anointing? Why this meal? Why the agony in the garden? Jesus knows the accusations are closing in, the Accuser is doing his worst. Judas, terribly, hands him over. The chief priests accuse him of many things, not realizing whose voice it is coming through their throats. They go on doing it the next morning, before Pilate. The crowds join in. Then the passers-by mock him, still accusing: Messiah, eh? Well, come down from the cross and then we'll believe you! The plots, the accusations, the Accuser. Jesus takes it all. It all comes on to him. This is central to Mark's meaning.

And then, flitting to and fro in the shadows of the story, the frightened characters who remind us so much of . . . well, of ourselves. The incomprehending disciples, not understanding about the ointment at Bethany. The worried disciples, each anxious that it might be him who would suddenly turn traitor. Blustering Peter, eager to swear that he'll stick it out, then collapsing like a pricked balloon when, for a moment, the searchlight of accusation swings round on to him. The soldiers, doing what (alas) soldiers still do, taking out their frustrations on an easy target. The bystanders, misunderstanding what Jesus is saying, watching and puzzling and only figuring it out long afterwards. The centurion, watching his thousandth victim die and suddenly realizing he'd never seen anything like this before.

The point is not to catch it all in a formula. The point is to stay there, to let the story wash over you again and again like a huge tidal wave, knocking you off your feet, rinsing you out, breaking you down, leaving you with nothing but awe and sorrow and gratitude and love. He did it for us. He did it for me. For you. For people near by and far away. Jesus has gone to the darkest place in the world, the place where all that he can say is 'My God, why did you abandon me?' And he has gone there, with all the plots and accusations and paranoia and frustration and hatred and misunderstanding and failed hopes and broken dreams of the world clattering about his head. He has gone there because that was, and is, the only way the world can be rescued. The only way you and I can be rescued. The only way by which God's love can take the worst on to itself and leave us free.

'This fellow really was God's son.' Mark tells us that the centurion was the first to say it. But he wants us to say it, too.

Today

Give us, almighty God, the faith and courage to stand this week at the foot of the cross, and to learn to see your glory there.

HOLY WEEK: PALM SUNDAY
Psalm 118.1–2, 19–29

¹O give thanks to the LORD, for he is good;
    his steadfast love endures for ever!

²Let Israel say,
    'His steadfast love endures for ever.'

¹⁹Open to me the gates of righteousness,
    that I may enter through them
    and give thanks to the LORD.

²⁰This is the gate of the LORD;
    the righteous shall enter through it.

²¹I thank you that you have answered me
    and have become my salvation.
²²The stone that the builders rejected
    has become the chief cornerstone.
²³This is the LORD's doing;
    it is marvellous in our eyes.
²⁴This is the day that the LORD has made;
    let us rejoice and be glad in it.
²⁵Save us, we beseech you, O LORD!
    O LORD, we beseech you, give us success!

²⁶Blessed is the one who comes in the name of the LORD.
   We bless you from the house of the LORD.
²⁷The LORD is God,
   and he has given us light.
Bind the festal procession with branches,
   up to the horns of the altar.

²⁸You are my God, and I will give thanks to you;
   you are my God, I will extol you.

²⁹O give thanks to the LORD, for he is good,
   for his steadfast love endures for ever.

The guests arrived on time, and soon the party was in full swing. The little nibbles, a whole variety of tasty little morsels, were delicious. The wine sparkled in the glasses. A lovely smell wafted through from the kitchen; clearly there was a major treat in store. The decorations made an already attractive room look like a fairy palace. How easy it was for the guests, enjoying one another's company and a good evening out, to take it all for granted.

I caught my wife's eye. Yes, it was good they were all here. We were glad to do it. But only she and I knew – and only she *really* knew – what it had taken to bring us to that point. The butcher had let us down, and an emergency dash to another shop had only just come up with the goods on time. The fridge hadn't been working properly, and she had worried all night that everything that should have been cold and crisp would be warm and soggy. I had blown the house's main fuse in putting up the extra lights. And in the middle of it all the key person who had kindly volunteered to help make all the little extras had gone down with the flu. The surface glitter of the party nicely covered over the days and hours when it felt as though we were pushing water uphill with our bare hands.

The problem of only reading verses 19–29 of this Psalm (yes: another complaint about the Lectionary!) is that it's like trying to get the party without the preparation. The party is great, but the preparation is what counts. Try to have the one without the other, and it's just not going to happen. (I am reminded of the story of the student phoning his mother to ask how to cook an elaborate dish, only to reveal, after she'd given him full instructions, that the guests were arriving in half an hour and he hadn't even done the shopping yet.) And the problem with the crowds on Palm Sunday was that they, like the Lectionary, wanted to get verses 19–29 without verses 5–18. Yes, the party will be wonderful: the gates of righteousness, the gate of the Lord, will open and let in the pilgrims; the rejected stone becomes the cornerstone; this is the day the Lord has made; blessed in the name of the Lord is the one who comes; give thanks to the Lord, for he is good, for his steadfast love endures for ever! Absolutely. That's God's party. That's what a genuine festival ought to look like and feel like. That's what the crowds at Passover time wanted, and they were right to want it.

But Jesus was living in verses 5–18. 'Out of my distress I called on the Lord.' 'It is better to take refuge in the Lord than to put confidence in princes.' 'I was pushed hard, so that I was falling, but the Lord helped me.' 'The Lord has punished me severely, but he did not give me over to death.' Except that Jesus went further and deeper. His preparation for the ultimate festival meant that, having taken refuge in the Lord, he ended up crying out that God had forsaken him. He put his confidence in the Lord, but the princes strung him up anyway. He was pushed hard, and fell, and nothing happened except more beating. He was punished severely, and he was indeed given over to death. The Psalmist knows that you only get to the joy of the festival by living through the pain and anguish of distress, opposition, danger and sorrow. Jesus knew that he would only arrive at it by drinking those horrible cups to the dregs.

Palm Sunday is therefore bound to be a bittersweet moment. Enjoy the moment of triumph and festival while it lasts, but recognize that it is only a foretaste of the real thing, and that you'll only get the real thing the other side of the pain, the

147

fear and the sense of abandonment. That was the problem in Jerusalem that day, as Jesus rode into the city with (so Luke tells us) tears rolling down his cheeks. He could see verses 5–18, not only for himself but for the whole city. He could see the nations surrounding Jerusalem, and Jerusalem not being able, in the name of the Lord, to cut them off. He could hear the glad songs of victory, not in the tents of the righteous, but in the pagan camp closing in on the city and Temple that had longed for the festival of freedom but had not been willing to embrace the necessary preparation.

Of course, for many Christians in Holy Week, the problem comes the other way round. Many are rightly concerned to keep Holy Week and Good Friday itself with proper solemnity, with a sorrowful awareness of the folly and sin to which we have all contributed and which put Jesus on the cross. Sometimes we are so good at all that that we forget about the festival. Let's keep the Psalm, and this coming week, in balance, and so prepare the ground by following Jesus all the way to Calvary that Easter, when it comes, will be the proper, thorough, well-grounded outburst of praise that it ought to be: the day the Lord has made, in which we will indeed rejoice and be glad.

Today

Teach us, good Lord, to share your journey of sorrow and pain, so that we may share the joy of your victory.

HOLY WEEK: MONDAY

Mark 14.3–9

³Jesus was in Bethany, at the house of Simon (known as 'the Leper'). While he was at table, a woman came up with an alabaster pot containing extremely valuable ointment made of pure spikenard. She broke the pot and poured the ointment on Jesus' head.

⁴Some of the people there grumbled to one another.

'What's the point of wasting the ointment?' they asked. ⁵'That ointment could have been sold for three hundred dinars, and given to the poor.'

And they were angry with her.

⁶'Leave her alone,' said Jesus. 'Why make trouble for her? She has done a wonderful thing for me. ⁷You have the poor with you always; you can help them whenever you want to. But you won't always have me.

⁸'She has played her part. She has anointed my body for its burial, ahead of time. ⁹I'm telling you the truth: wherever the message is announced in all the world, the story of what she has just done will be told. That will be her memorial.'

How much did you earn last year?

Or, if you don't earn a regular wage, how much did it cost you to live last year?

Think about that sum for a moment. Now imagine that someone who had that amount of money sitting in the bank decided to spend it all on a wonderful gift for you and your family. A magnificent set of china and silver, perhaps. Wonderful new furniture for the whole house. An entire library of all your favourite books (or, if you're not into books, of DVDs – films, TV programmes, the lot). You can hardly imagine what a wonderful gift you would be given.

And now imagine that a member of your family had just met someone they considered utterly wonderful. Someone with such a combination of gentle wisdom, powerful insight, holiness and happiness, that simply to be in his presence was a privilege beyond words. And this family member decided, without telling the rest of you, to turn that wonderful gift back into cash and give it all to this strange new friend.

What would you think? What would you feel?

You would feel, and think, exactly what the people in verse 4 felt and thought. Ointment worth three hundred dinars: a dinar was roughly a day's wage for an ordinary labourer, so allowing for days off and holidays three hundred of them might well be about a year's worth. And there it was, a wonderful jar of ointment, far beyond the reach of the poor people in Bethany (the word 'Bethany' means 'House of the Poor', and it's possible that there was a community there that looked after the poor).

And Mary (Mark doesn't name her, but John does in 11.2 and 12.3) takes this ointment and pours it all over Jesus. The smell is wonderful, filling the whole house.

So they grumble. Of course they do. Their heads are down, looking at the immediate problems that most people in the world face every day: how to get through tomorrow, next week, next month. No money to spare, no time to stop and think about larger issues. And none of them have been paying attention to what Jesus has been telling them for the last few weeks. *This week is when it must happen. This is the moment when the son of man will be handed over and killed.*

Did Mary reflect on that? Probably not. She acted out of love and gratitude, her intuition leaping over the prudential reasoning of the grumblers all around. But Jesus took her intuitive generosity and interpreted it in a new, dark and powerful way. 'She has anointed my body for its burial, ahead of time.' Jesus can see, already, what lies ahead: a horrible death, a quick burial, no time for niceties. So the anointing has been done already, in advance.

But there is more. As Jesus goes to his death, with his disciples still unaware of what he's thinking, he looks beyond: to a message of good news going out into all the world. 'Wherever the message is announced in all the world,' he says (verse 9), 'the story of what she has just done will be told. That will be her memorial.' The 'message' here is the 'good news', the 'gospel' which announces Jesus as king, king of Israel and king of the world. James and John wanted to make sure they got the best seats in the kingdom. They were given no such promises. Mary, acting out of selfless generosity, is promised something better: an honoured place in the story, as long as the world hears the gospel. And there she still is.

Meanwhile, the intuitive generosity (which of course reflects the same quality in God) must also concern itself with the practical needs all around. 'You have the poor with you always; you can help them whenever you want to.' This statement is not designed as a shrug of the shoulders, an excuse for rich people to say that, since there will always be poor people, we don't have to help them out of their poverty. It is making a quite astonishing claim: that service to Jesus himself ranks before service even to the poor. Love God with all your heart, mind, soul and strength, said Jesus, summing up the ancient law, and your neighbour as yourself. Hidden at the heart of this powerful little drama, capturing as it does several deep human emotions, is the claim that service rendered to Jesus is part of the first commandment, not as an excuse for avoiding the second but as a matter of getting priorities straightened out.

Today

Give us, loving Lord, such love for you that our generosity will overflow whenever you need it.

HOLY WEEK: TUESDAY

Mark 14.32–52

³²They came to a place called Gethsemane.

'Stay here', said Jesus to the disciples, 'while I pray.'

³³He took Peter, James and John with him, and became quite overcome and deeply distressed.

³⁴"My soul is disturbed within me", he said, 'right to the point of death. Stay here and keep watch.'

³⁵He went a little further, and fell on the ground and prayed that, if possible, the moment might pass from him.

³⁶'Abba, father,' he said, 'all things are possible for you! Take this cup away from me! But – not what I want, but what you want.'

[37]He returned and found them sleeping.

'Are you asleep, Simon?' he said to Peter. 'Couldn't you keep watch for a single hour? [38]Watch and pray, so that you won't come into the time of trouble. The spirit is eager, but the body is weak.'

[39]Once more he went off and prayed, saying the same words. [40]And again, when he returned, he found them asleep, because their eyes were very heavy. They had no words to answer him. [41]But the third time he came, he said to them, 'All right – sleep as much as you like now. Have a good rest. The job is done, the time has come – and look! The son of man is betrayed into the clutches of sinners. [42]Get up, let's be on our way. Here comes the man who's going to betray me.'

[43]At once, while he was still speaking, Judas, one of the Twelve, arrived, accompanied by a crowd, with swords and clubs, from the chief priests, the legal experts, and the elders. [44]The betrayer had given them a coded sign: 'The one I kiss – that's him! Seize him and take him away safely.'

[45]He came up to Jesus at once. 'Rabbi!' he said, and kissed him.

[46]The crowd laid hands on him and seized him. [47]One of the bystanders drew a sword and struck the high priest's servant, cutting off his ear. [48]Then Jesus spoke to them.

'Anyone would think', he said, 'you'd come after a brigand! Fancy needing swords and clubs to arrest me! [49]Day after day I've been teaching in the Temple, under your noses, and you never laid a finger on me. But the scriptures must be fulfilled.'

[50]Then they all abandoned him and ran away.

[51]A young man had followed him, wearing only a linen tunic over his otherwise naked body. [52]They seized him, and he left the tunic and ran away naked.

Two generations ago, J. B. Phillips (best known for his translation of the New Testament) published a little book called *Your God Is Too Small*. It was a moving appeal for ordinary Christians to lift up their eyes and imaginations, and to realize that God is not simply a therapist, concerned with the humdrum, day-to-day matters of their personal lives and problems, but is the glorious sovereign of heaven and earth. We all need that kind of reminder on a regular basis.

But there is, perhaps, a more subtle point which needs to be made as well. When people start to get the point about the sovereignty, majesty and glory of the one true God, it is often difficult for them at the same time to glimpse and grasp the real divine greatness which the gospel stories reveal. But if we don't get this point, as well as the larger one, we will fall back once more into the mistake of James and John, celebrating the greatness of God and hoping that some of that greatness will rub off on us in the usual, worldly sense.

All along in Mark's book we have seen that Jesus is described as the one who, however surprisingly, is fulfilling the promises that Israel's God will come back to his people at last, rescuing them and filling the world with his glory. Think back to the opening scene. Here is the preparatory messenger, here is the voice in the wilderness, and now here is the Coming One: my son, my beloved one, the one who makes me glad. Somehow, already, we have to get our heads around what Mark is saying: God promised that he would come back, but the one who's come is Jesus, and Jesus is hailed by God himself as his beloved son.

Mark offers no theory about how this makes sense. The earliest Christians didn't theorize: they worshipped. They remained firmly monotheistic: Jesus wasn't a 'second god' added to the one they'd already got. But, somehow, they found that worshipping Jesus and worshipping the one whom Jesus called 'father' went together.

We might, as I say, just about be getting our heads and our hearts around this. But the scene we now witness strains this picture in a new way. It offers a whole new dimension of the word 'God' itself. Gethsemane stands at the heart of the whole early Christian picture of who God is, and hence of who we ourselves (bearing God's image) are meant to be. And at the heart of Gethsemane there stands the unforgettable prayer

153

that shows what love really means, the love that passes between father and son, the love that reaches out to this day into the dark places of the world: 'Abba, father,' he said, 'all things are possible for you! Take this cup away from me! But – not what I want, but what you want.'

Not long ago, I heard a church leader declare that with this passage we actually see 'conflict' within the Trinity itself. (He was using this idea to justify continuing conflict within the church.) But Gethsemane is not about conflict. It is about love. This is the full, honest interchange of love in which the son lays before the father the true condition of his God-reflecting humanity, caught now in the necessary work of bearing the utter pain and sorrow of the world.

But, people might say, doesn't this prayer show that Jesus and his father are, as it were, on opposite sides of the equation? Doesn't it appear that Jesus wants to be released from his obligation, but knows that the father wills it anyway?

Not so fast. What Jesus' prayer shows is the proper, right, natural reaction of any human being, and particularly the human being who completely reflected the life-giving God, to the dark forces of corruption and death. It shows that as Jesus went to the cross he was not doing it out of a distorted death-wish, a kind of crazy suicide mission. He continued, as one would expect from the life-restoring son of the life-giving father, to resist death with every fibre of his being. His very prayer to be rescued from it displays not a resistance to the father's will, but a resistance to the forces of evil which result in death. There is no conflict here; only the deepest affirmation of the father's will in all its aspects.

And now we ask again: is your God *this* big? Big enough to come and take on the forces of evil and death *by dying under their weight and power*? There's a hymn which has a verse beginning, 'Jesus is Lord! Yet from his throne eternal, in flesh he came to die in shame on Calvary's tree.' There is one word there that is wrong. It shouldn't be 'yet'. It should be 'so'. Jesus is Lord, *and so, and therefore*, he came into the world, came to his own people, came to the place of fear and horror and shame and guilt and evil and darkness and death itself. He came out of love, love for the father, love for the world. That is what Mark's story is telling us. All the theologians down the centuries have produced formulae to explain this. But it's all here, in a nutshell, within this astonishing story.

And of course the disciples didn't get it. First they fall asleep. Then they make a half-baked attempt to defend Jesus. And then – many people think this is Mark's own signature, a shocking and shaming personal memory – one young man is grabbed by the tunic, so leaves the tunic and runs away naked. That says it all. Humankind, naked and ashamed in the garden, while the snake closes in for the kill. The son of man has arrived at the place where the problem began, to take its full force upon himself.

Today

Lord Jesus, King and Master, help us to watch with you, to stay with you, to learn from your anguish the lessons of love.

HOLY WEEK: WEDNESDAY
Mark 14.53–65

[53]They took Jesus away to the high priest. All the chief priests and the elders and legal experts were assembled. [54]Peter followed him at a distance, and came to the courtyard of the high priest's house, where he sat with the servants and warmed himself at the fire.

[55]The chief priests, and all the Sanhedrin, looked for evidence for a capital charge against Jesus, but they didn't find any. [56]Several people invented fictitious charges against him, but their evidence didn't agree. [57]Then some stood up with this fabricated charge: [58]"We heard him say, "I will destroy this

Temple, which human hands have made, and in three days I'll build another, made without human hands."'

[59]But even so their evidence didn't agree.

[60]Then the high priest got up in front of them all and interrogated Jesus.

'Haven't you got any answer about whatever it is these people are testifying against you?'

[61]Jesus remained silent, and didn't answer a word.

Once more the high priest questioned him.

'Are you the Messiah, the Son of the Blessed One?'

[62]'I am,' replied Jesus, 'and you will see "the son of man sitting at the right hand of Power, and coming with the clouds of heaven".'

[63]'Why do we need any more evidence?' shouted the high priest, tearing his clothes. [64]'You heard the blasphemy! What's your verdict?'

They all agreed on their judgment: he deserved to die.

[65]Some of them began to spit at him. They blindfolded him and hit him, and said, 'Prophesy!' And the servants took charge of him and beat him.

I remember as a child being fascinated with some really old Russian dolls. Made out of thin wood, they came apart in the middle with a satisfying squeak, revealing a smaller one inside. Then the next, and the next. Eventually you reach the smallest, a tiny little doll still perfectly formed and painted. You can, of course, set them alongside one another on the mantelpiece. But you can also put them back together and enjoy the knowledge of what's hidden inside the one you can still see.

Many years later I came upon a set of Russian dolls that made a quirky political point. It was while Mikhail Gorbachev was in charge of the old Soviet Union, at the time when it was undergoing its astonishing transformation. So the outer doll, the biggest one in the collection, was Gorbachev himself. Inside him was Chernenko, and inside him Andropov (neither of whom ruled for very long). Inside Andropov was Brezhnev, one of the key figures in the cold war of the 1960s and 70s. Inside Brezhnev was Khrushchev, whom I remember from my young days. And inside Khrushchev (missing out Malenkov, a short-term and forgettable Soviet leader in the early 1950s) was the old man himself, Joseph Stalin, responsible for the deaths of tens of millions of his own people. The point was starkly clear: they're basically all the same. Open up one and you'll find the others.

Now there are two ways in which that illustration can help us into a fuller understanding of what's going on in this dense and frightening scene, the confrontation between Jesus and the high priest. First, let's open up the high priest himself, and see what we find inside.

Caiaphas was part of the ruling elite, the wealthy Jerusalem-based aristocracy. He was a politician to his fingertips, who knew all the dodges and tricks to try to balance out what Rome expected of local leaders on the one hand and what the ordinary people expected of their priests on the other. He could of course take the high moral and theological ground at the drop of a hat, as he does when he shouts 'blasphemy' and tears his clothes as a sign of his supposed horror at such a thing (in fact, Mark is telling us, he was delighted: Jesus had just handed him the result he wanted).

Any first-century Jew would have told you that Caiaphas was just like all his predecessors: heavily compromised, out for his own ends, staying in power at whatever cost there might be to everyone else and to the integrity of Judaism. Open him up, and you'll find a string of other time-serving leaders going back several centuries, far longer than the leaders of Communist Russia.

But Mark is interested in going back another stage behind this. When Jesus gives his final answer, he quotes from Daniel 7: 'you will see "the son of man sitting at the right hand of Power, and coming with the clouds of heaven".' Go back to Daniel 7 and see: when 'one like a son of man' is seen 'coming with the clouds of heaven' (7.13, NIV) this is the heart of *a great court scene in which God himself is vindicating his people* against the wicked attacks of the monsters who have opposed and oppressed them. Now here, Mark is saying, is this great court scene, the climax of the gospel so far. *And Caiaphas is cast in the role of the fourth and final monster*, perhaps even the 'little horn' of Daniel 7.19–22. Even if we think it likely that Mark envisages Rome itself as the 'fourth monster' in Daniel's scheme, Caiaphas is here acting as chief spokesman. Open him up, and instead of the wise, devout leader of God's people, we see the blasphemous, arrogant opponent of God's kingdom.

Now try the same with Jesus. Throughout the gospel he has been seen as a prophet (6.15; 8.28). Now he's accused of being a *false* prophet, announcing the destruction and rebuilding of the Temple (verses 57–58). That's why, when they decide he's guilty, the mocking crowd gather round, blindfold him, and invite him to 'prophesy', guessing who has been hitting him. (Meanwhile, as Mark's reader then discovers, Jesus' prophecy about Peter denying him is coming true.)

But, though being a false prophet (and speaking against the Temple) was a serious and possibly fatal charge, Caiaphas opens up the first Russian doll and peers inside. If you're making claims about destroying and rebuilding the Temple, does that mean you think you're the Messiah? It is, after all, the Messiah who has the rights over the Temple, ever since David planned it and Solomon built it.

Caiaphas here thinks of messiahship simply in terms of human kingship. But this time it is Jesus, and then Mark telling the story, who open the disguise still further. Yes, Jesus is a prophet, a true prophet. Yes, he is the Messiah, the one who has the right to declare the Temple redundant and to promise a God-given replacement. But inside this he is much, much more. He is the one who will be exalted, after his suffering, to sit 'at the right hand of Power', that is, of God.

Jesus has here combined Daniel 7 with Psalm 110.1, which became a favourite text in the early Christian movement (and which he'd already used to baffle his questioners in 12.35–37). He has discovered in the scriptures the two texts which speak most plainly of the fact that, when Israel's representative has completed his appointed task, he will take his rightful place beside God himself, sharing as it were the very throne of God, or perhaps sitting on a second throne right beside him. This is where we discover the secret that lay behind that dialogue of love and agony in the garden of Gethsemane. This is where we learn that within the profiles of 'prophet' and 'Messiah' there is a hidden, secret identity. Now at last, now when it can no longer be misunderstood in terms of self-serving power, now when he is bound to be misunderstood and when his judges are bound to find him guilty – now at last Jesus can do what God himself does at the moment of the Exodus (Exodus 3.13–15). Now at last he can reveal who he really is. 'This is our God, the Servant King.'

Today

Lord Jesus, king and master: guiltless, you were condemned; life-giver, you were sent to death; lover of all, you were hated and mocked. We worship you and we bless your name.

HOLY WEEK: MAUNDY THURSDAY
Mark 14.12–26

[12]On the first day of unleavened bread, when the Passover lambs were sacrificed, Jesus' disciples said to him, 'Where would you like us to go and get things ready for you to eat the Passover?'

[13]He sent off two of his disciples, with these instructions.

'Go into the city, and you will be met by a man carrying a water-pot. Follow him. [14]When he goes indoors, say to the master of the house, "The teacher says, where is the guest room for me, where I can eat the Passover with my disciples?"

[15]He will show you a large upstairs room, set out and ready. Make preparations for us there.'

[16]The disciples went out, entered the city, and found it exactly as he had said. They prepared the Passover.

[17]When it was evening, Jesus came with the Twelve. [18]As they were reclining at table and eating, Jesus said, 'I'm telling you the truth: one of you is going to betray me – one of you that's eating with me.'

[19]They began to be very upset, and they said to him, one after another, 'It isn't me, is it?'

[20]'It's one of the Twelve,' said Jesus, 'one who has dipped his bread in the dish with me. [21]Yes: the son of man is completing his journey, as scripture said he would; but it's bad news for the man who betrays him! It would have been better for that man never to have been born.'

[22]While they were eating, he took bread, blessed it, broke it, and gave it to them.

'Take it,' he said. 'This is my body.'

[23]Then he took the cup, gave thanks, and gave it to them, and they all drank from it.

[24]'This is my blood of the covenant,' he said, 'which is poured out for many. [25]I'm telling you the truth: I won't ever drink from the fruit of the vine again, until that day – the day when I drink it new in the kingdom of God.'

[26]They sang a hymn, and went out to the Mount of Olives.

When I taught in Oxford University, I used repeatedly to ask the Theology Faculty for funds to take students to the Holy Land. Having been there myself, I knew that you could learn things in a few days on site that would take you several weeks in the library and classroom.

My superiors disagreed. There are plenty of books in the library, they said, with maps and pictures and full descriptions. You don't need to go there yourself.

Only a library-bound academic, of course, could think like that. Most people find that, when they go to the Holy Land, scales fall from their eyes. The sights. The sounds. The smells. The people. The meals.

The meals! Yes, indeed. Sharing a meal is one of the most ordinary and at the same time one of the most profound things we humans ever do. As I write this I am expecting to have lunch by myself, and I feel that as a deprivation, a loss. Meals bind us together. They say something about who we are, and why. Though fewer people in my country now enjoy the traditional family Sunday lunch, those who do are dimly aware that such an event is just as much about 'family' and 'Sunday' as it is about 'lunch'. Events, particularly the event of a meal, convey meaning far more powerfully than any words, any books, any theories.

And Jesus chose a meal, a particular meal, to convey the deepest meaning of all. The reason why he was going to die.

It was a Passover meal – of a sort. Clearly it *was* a Passover meal; Mark is quite explicit. And Jesus, having chosen to come to Jerusalem on this Passover to make his dramatic move in the Temple and take the consequences, was likely (knowing all we know of him) to choose, as well, to focus the dense, multi-layered meaning of his final hours on an event like this. It was to be an event that his followers would be able to repeat, and, in so doing, find again and again his meaning, his life, his presence.

But it was a Passover meal with a difference. Passover meals look back to the Exodus from Egypt, and celebrate the fact that God rescued his people from slavery and constituted them as his free people – even though, for much of their history, the Jewish people have continued to suffer slavery, exile and oppression. Jesus' special meal looked back like that, but it also looked on to a further event: the coming of God's kingdom. Jesus was looking forward to the next time he would drink wine with his followers: by then, the kingdom would have come (verse 25). As we have seen several times already, this can only mean, as Mark draws out, that Jesus saw his approaching death as the means by which that kingdom would be established.

In particular, of course, Jesus, playing host for the meal, makes a startling alteration in some of the basic words that the host has to speak. No longer is the bread they share a reminder of the bread of affliction in Egypt. It is his body. No longer is the wine the celebration of God's ancient rescue operation. It is his blood: 'the blood of the covenant' (another echo of the Exodus story), 'poured out for many' (an ancient Jewish way of saying 'for the whole people'). This meal declares, from that first Maundy Thursday onwards, that those who share it are God's new-covenant people, the restored and renewed Israel, and that they are this because, and only because, of Jesus' forthcoming death. There are things that you can learn from sharing in this meal, wherever and however you do it, which you couldn't learn no matter how long you sat in the library or how many books you read.

In particular, we learn from Mark's description of this meal that we can never take part in it lightly or casually. It is fatally easy for Christians, as St Paul already found out in Corinth, to come to the family meal in an easy-going fashion, without really thinking out what's going on and hence what sort of people we should be. When Jesus himself led that Passover celebration, he was aware of a snake in the grass. A betrayer, at the table with him. Mark, as so often, folds the story together in such a way that the middle bit, in this case the prediction of the betrayal, is held in tension between the outer bits, the preparation of the meal and then the meal itself. Somehow, Mark is saying, the forthcoming betrayal is itself part of the meaning.

When we break bread together ourselves, in other words – whether we call it 'the Eucharist' or 'the Mass', or 'the Lord's Supper' or 'Holy Communion', or simply 'the bread-breaking', it's all the same – we do so in the knowledge that at the heart of every Christian community, and at the heart of every Christian individual, there lies the capacity for betrayal. We keep this festival solemnly, humbly, seeking for mercy and courage and strength, not with a casual cheerfulness that thinks of the meal as a piece of magic which gets round the need for serious spiritual and moral self-examination. Sharing a meal with any friend is a good and powerful thing to do. Sharing a meal – sharing *this* meal of meals – with Jesus, the meal in which he gives himself to his people and enables them to eat and drink all the meaning of his forthcoming death, is an event so full of meaning that the words run out long before it's done. Beware the rationalism that takes the Word made Flesh and insists on turning it back again into mere words.

Today

Teach us, good Lord, so to share your table that we may be loyal to you for ever, come what may.

HOLY WEEK: GOOD FRIDAY

Mark 15.1–41

[1]As soon as morning came, the chief priests held a council meeting with the elders, the legal experts, and the whole Sanhedrin. They bound Jesus, took him off to Pilate, and handed him over.

[2]'Are you the king of the Jews?' asked Pilate.

'You have said it,' replied Jesus.

[3]The chief priests laid many accusations against him.

[4]Pilate again interrogated him: 'Aren't you going to make any reply? Look how many things they're accusing you of!'

[5]But Jesus gave no reply at all, which astonished Pilate.

[6]The custom was that at festival time he used to release for them a single prisoner, whoever they would ask for. [7]There was a man in prison named Barabbas, one of the revolutionaries who had committed murder during the uprising. [8]So the crowd came up and began to ask Pilate to do what he normally did.

[9]'Do you want me', answered Pilate, 'to release for you "the king of the Jews"?'

¹⁰He said this because he knew that the chief priests had handed him over out of envy. ¹¹The chief priests stirred up the crowd to ask for Barabbas instead to be released to them. So Pilate once again asked them, ¹²'What then do you want me to do with the one you call "the king of the Jews"?'

¹³'Crucify him!' they shouted again.

¹⁴'Why?' asked Pilate. 'What has he done wrong?'

'Crucify him!' they shouted all the louder.

¹⁵Pilate wanted to satisfy the crowd; so he released Barabbas for them. He had Jesus flogged, and handed him over to be crucified.

¹⁶The soldiers took Jesus into the courtyard, that is, the Praetorium, and called together the whole squad. ¹⁷They dressed Jesus up in purple; then, weaving together a crown of thorns, they stuck it on him. ¹⁸They began to salute him: 'Greetings, King of the Jews!' ¹⁹And they hit him over the head with a staff, and spat at him, and knelt down to do him homage. ²⁰Then, when they had mocked him, they took the purple robe off him, and put his own clothes back on.

Then they led him off to crucify him. ²¹They compelled a man called Simon to carry Jesus' cross. He was from Cyrene, and was coming in from out of town. He was the father of Alexander and Rufus.

²²They took Jesus to the place called Golgotha, which in translation means 'Skull's Place'. ²³They gave him a mixture of wine and myrrh, but he didn't drink it.

²⁴So they crucified him; they 'parted his clothing between them, casting lots' to see who would get what. ²⁵It was about nine o'clock in the morning when they crucified him. ²⁶The inscription, giving the charge, read: 'The King of the Jews'. ²⁷They also crucified two bandits alongside him, one on his right and one on his left.

²⁹People who were passing by abused him. They shook their heads at him.

'Hah!' they said. 'You were going to destroy the Temple, were you? And build it again in three days? ³⁰Why don't you rescue yourself, and come down from the cross?'

³¹The chief priests and the lawyers were mocking him in the same way among themselves.

'He rescued others,' they said, 'but he can't rescue himself. ³²Messiah, is he? King of Israel, did he say? Well, let's see him come down from the cross! We'll believe him when we see that!'

The two who were crucified alongside him taunted him as well.

³³At midday there was darkness over all the land until three in the afternoon. ³⁴At three o'clock Jesus shouted out in a powerful voice, '*Eloi, Eloi, lema sabachthani?*' which means, 'My God, my God, why did you abandon me?'

³⁵When the bystanders heard it, some of them said, 'He's calling for Elijah!'

³⁶One of them ran and filled a sponge with sour wine, put it on a pole, and gave it him to drink.

'Well then,' he declared, 'let's see if Elijah will come and take him down.'

³⁷But Jesus, with another loud shout, breathed his last.

³⁸The Temple veil was torn in two, from top to bottom. ³⁹When the centurion who was standing facing him saw that he died in this way, he said, 'This fellow really was God's son.'

⁴⁰Some women were watching from a distance. They included Mary Magdalene, Mary the mother of the younger James and of Joses, and Salome. ⁴¹They had followed Jesus in Galilee, and had attended to his needs. There were several other women, too, who had come up with him to Jerusalem.

We stopped the car outside the most unlikely looking house. One wall looked as if it was going to collapse at any moment. The door was hanging off on one hinge. An upstairs window was broken. There was a rustle in the bushes nearby, as though we had interrupted a rodent in its afternoon work. Could this really be the place?

We thought back through the last hour of the drive. We had followed all the signposts. We had taken all the turns. We had checked the mileage. There was no other house in sight. This must be the place. But . . . why?

The resolution of that story must wait for another time. But unless we feel something of that same sense of horror and bafflement as we read Mark 15, we are missing the point. We have followed all the signposts, from the voice at Jesus' baptism through Peter's blurting out that Jesus was the Messiah, through all the events of Jesus' early public career, through the transfiguration, right up to the triumphal entry into Jerusalem with the crowds hailing him as king, and then, dramatically and ironically, Caiaphas asking if Jesus really was the Messiah and Jesus saying yes, and much more. He's the king! He's the Messiah! He's the one Israel has been waiting for! We've taken all the right turnings. We've checked our calculations. This must be the moment. There is nobody else in sight. Either he's the Messiah or nobody is.

But . . . why? Why is he collapsing under the weight of the cross? Why is he hanging there on that cross? Why is his body broken, his head bleeding, his limbs pulled roughly apart and nailed to a plank? And what about those scavengers, the rats, the dogs, the birds, circling around and scenting carrion? How can this be the climax to the royal story, to Israel's story, to the story of God's kingdom coming on earth as in heaven?

Perhaps we've made a mistake? Perhaps the 'royal' theme was only a feature of the earlier story, and perhaps Mark is now moving on to something else? No. Look through it again. 'Are you the king of the Jews?' 'Do you want me to release for you "the king of the Jews"?' 'What shall I do with the one you call "the king of the Jews"?' 'Greetings, King of the Jews!' 'The inscription read: "The King of the Jews".' 'Messiah, is he? King of Israel, did he say?' And then – echoing all the way back to the royal announcement at the baptism – 'This fellow really was God's son.' No mistake. This is what Mark is telling us. This is where the king comes into his own, enthroned (as he warned James and John) with one on his right and the other on his left.

So what sense does it make?

Mark must mean, somehow, that this is how, finally, God was establishing his kingdom through Jesus and his work. He must mean that this is the event that made sense of all those advance signs of the kingdom – the healings, the exorcisms, the multiplication of loaves, and so on. This is the event that declared that God was God, that he was picking up the reins of power to rule on earth as in heaven. It must mean that. It can only mean that.

But it must, then, mean that the very nature of power, of God's exercise of power, of the power that rules the world, has been so radically redefined that most people simply wouldn't recognize it. As Isaiah said, who would have believed that he was 'the Arm of the Lord' (53.1)? This isn't what power looks like in our world. Pontius Pilate is the one (surely, we think) who shows us what power looks like. But no: this was the whole point of Jesus' answer to James and John, ending with his own reference to Isaiah 53. Power has been turned upside down. One wise old writer commented, thinking of St Paul's eventual trial before Nero, that the time would come when people would call their sons 'Paul' and their dogs 'Nero'. In the same way, the only thing people tend to know about Pilate today is that (in one of the other accounts) he washed his hands to signify innocence when in fact he was horribly guilty: not only guilty, in other words, but devious. Nobody sings hymns to Pilate, or offers him their love and allegiance.

But Jesus? It is, of course, the crucified Jesus who has drawn to himself people of all sorts, especially people in dire need. Countless thousands have read this story and have seen their own story mirrored in it: their own tale of injustice, their own horrible betrayal, their own false accusation, their own unjustified humiliation, their own suffering, their own death.

So how does it then 'work'? All those theories about the meaning of the cross, the theories that have concentrated on Jesus standing in for us and taking what we deserved, have always run the risk of sounding both mechanical and, in themselves, somehow unfair. If you reduce the whole thing to a legalistic punishment which Jesus takes so we don't, you have scaled the whole thing right down to a point, and (what's more) a point which many, quite understandably, find either puzzling or repelling.

But widen the scale again. Let your eyes scan the entire horizon of Mark 15, revealing as it does the place where God's people were in pain, the place where the whole world was in pain. The tectonic plates of the moral universe ground together in the Middle East, producing this massive clash of empires and aspirations, of hopes and fears, of injustice and accusation and horror and misery. Let your gaze take all that in, and then see the truth of which that narrowly defined formula ('we deserve punishment; Jesus takes it instead') is simply one focal point.

The great truth is this: that the one who embodied Israel's God, coming in person to rescue and rule, came to the point where the pain of the world, and of Israel, was most sharply focused, and took it upon himself. Those countless thousands could most likely not explain why they somehow knew this. They might well not have realized that Israel was designed, in God's plan, to represent humanity and the world, and that Jesus, as Messiah, was called to represent Israel. That is, so to speak, how it 'works'. But that's not necessarily how the story 'works' on those who read it. As John Bunyan said, it was a great mystery to him why the sight of the cross should so ease him of his burden. But ease him it did.

Today

Were the whole realm of nature mine, that were an offering far too small; Love so amazing, so divine, demands my soul, my life, my all.

HOLY WEEK: HOLY SATURDAY
Mark 15.42–47

[42]It was already getting towards evening, and it was the day of Preparation, that is, the day before the sabbath. [43]Joseph of Arimathea, a reputable member of the Council who was himself eagerly awaiting God's kingdom, took his courage in both hands, went to Pilate, and requested the body of Jesus.

[44]Pilate was surprised that he was already dead. He summoned the centurion, and asked whether he had been dead for some time. [45]When he learned the facts from the centurion, he conceded the body to Joseph.

[46]So Joseph bought a linen cloth, took the body down, wrapped it in the cloth, and laid it in a tomb cut out of the rock. He rolled a stone against the door of the tomb. [47]Mary Magdalene and Mary the mother of Joses saw where he was buried.

It is hard to tell which was more horrible. We watched on the television, some while ago now, as the earthquake off the coast of Japan produced a terrible tsunami. The waves came crashing in, the enormous power of millions of tons of water carrying houses, buses, railway trains, anything and everything in its deadly path. It would have been exciting and dramatic if it had not been so nightmarish.

But then, after the storm, the calm. Not the calm of respite, of waking up and discovering it had all been a bad dream. Not the calm of a flat sea after the ship has weathered the high winds and waves. The broken, twisted calm of a landscape destroyed beyond recognition. Of people walking aimlessly to and fro, unable even to imagine where to begin to clean up, to clear up, to rebuild lives and communities. Our hearts and prayers went out to those people, and they still do.

Holy Saturday must have been like that. Any bereavement leaves you numb, squashed under the heavy, choking cloud of grief. This was a bereavement like no other. For Jesus' followers, it was as though they had waited all day for a drink of pure, cold water, and then, when they were lifting the cup to their lips, it was snatched from them and splashed on the dusty ground. It was like the woman who waits through the war for her husband to return, only to have him killed in a car accident a street away from home. It was like the child who returns home after a hard day at school and finds the parents vanished, and hard, rough strangers in the house instead. It was all of this and much, much more. Not only was Jesus dead. Dead! How could he be? But he was. But, almost as bad, looming up like a further great, dark wave, the sense of impossibility, of hopelessness, of a future not just blank but full of nothing but horror. Jesus was the last best hope. And he was dead.

Many have explored this Holy Saturday moment and found in it a strange sort of comfort. It's all about waiting; and part of the point of the waiting is not knowing what's going to come next, as certainly Jesus' followers did not know. Jesus had, to be sure, tried on several occasions to explain to them that he was going to die, *and to be raised.* But they hadn't understood this, just as they hadn't understood when he told them to keep quiet about the transfiguration 'until the son of man has been raised from the dead'. They wondered then what this 'rising from the dead' might mean; as far as they were concerned 'the resurrection' was something that would happen to everybody at the end of time, not something that would happen to one person in the middle of time.

So nobody was going around, that first Holy Saturday, saying 'never mind; in a couple of days he'll be back'. If they could say anything at all, through their tears and the cold, hard fear that must have gripped them all, it will have been to express a baffled hopelessness. How could they have been so wrong as to think of Jesus as Messiah? But surely they couldn't have been wrong; nobody had ever done things like that, nobody had ever spoken like that, nobody had ever loved like that. But they must have been wrong. He died, they crucified him, that doesn't happen to God's Messiah. And so on, round and round the miserable tracks.

Meanwhile, one brave man does what one brave man can do. Joseph of Arimathea uses his official status as a Council member in the service of his unofficial status as a kingdom-sympathizer. He does for Jesus what gentle friendship can still do. The two Marys see where Jesus is buried. There is a sense of sad quietness about it all.

Yes: like the sad quietness in so many human tragedies and injustices. Holy Saturday gives us a particular kind of space, if we are prepared to take it amid what is often a busy weekend. Holy Saturday offers at least a small moment in which the terrible, blinding truth of Good Friday can sink down into our bones and bloodstream and enable us to make it our own, rather than blundering on as though it hadn't quite happened. Holy Saturday can be the moment, if we will let it, when the warm clay of our lives, which has been stamped with the cross on Good Friday, sets firm, so that we become people of the cross, people who see the world in the light of the cross, people who, like Paul, have been crucified with the Messiah, so that the life they now live is not their own but his. Like Joseph, we have to take our courage in both hands if we are to do so. But this is the only way to go. We cannot be Easter people if we are not first Good Friday people and then Holy Saturday people. Don't expect even a still, small voice. Stay still yourself, and let the quietness and darkness of the day be your only companions.

Today

Jesus is dead. Jesus is dead. Think of a world where Jesus is dead.

EASTER DAY
Mark 16.1–8

¹When the sabbath was over, Mary Magdalene, Mary the mother of James, and Salome bought spices so that they could come

and anoint Jesus. [2]Then, very early on the first day of the week, they came to the tomb, just at sunrise. [3]They were saying to one another, 'There's that stone at the door of the tomb – who's going to roll it away for us?'

[4]Then, when they looked up, they saw that it had been rolled away. (It was extremely large.)

[5]So they went into the tomb, and there they saw a young man sitting on the right-hand side. He was wearing white. They were totally astonished.

[6]'Don't be astonished,' he said to them. 'You're looking for Jesus the Nazarene, who was crucified. He has been raised! He isn't here! Look – this is the place where they laid him.

[7]'But go and tell his disciples – including Peter – that he is going ahead of you to Galilee. You'll see him there, just like he told you.'

[8]They went out, and fled from the tomb. Trembling and panic had seized them. They said nothing to anyone, because they were afraid.

'They said nothing to anyone, because they were afraid.' Well, wouldn't you be? Terrified, more likely. Graveyards are a bad enough place at the best of times, especially in a culture where grave-robbery was common, and stories of ghosts, hauntings and other spooky events even more common. And when you belong to the small group that had gone around with the leader the authorities caught and executed two or three days earlier, you had to be extra careful. Afraid? You bet.

People today are afraid of Easter for totally different reasons. Well, perhaps not totally different. The gatekeepers of 'modern' Western society have decreed that religion is dangerous nonsense; that if there is a 'god' he's a long way away and only interested in your private spiritual life; that Progress, Technology and 'Science' (by which they mean not real science, the delighted and humble exploration of the universe, but an ideology that uses the same name) are in charge, and taking us towards a golden future. And that dead people do not rise.

They have to add that last bit, of course – not that it's a new idea. Homer knew that the dead don't rise. Pliny, the great Roman naturalist, was well aware of it too. That's hardly surprising, since it is the universal human experience. Dead people stay dead. The early Christians knew that too, and that was why what they discovered on that first Easter morning blew their minds and imaginations. They weren't ignorant folk who didn't know 'the laws of nature'. But those who try to shape today's Western world-view insist on 'no resurrection' for the same reason as all other totalizing systems insist on it. If Jesus was raised from the dead, a new power has been let loose in the world, a power which goes beyond all other power known to the human race. All other power, in the last analysis, ends up killing people. That's the bottom line. But if there is a God who raises the dead, all other powers are called to account. Resurrection challenges human empire where it hurts most. Hence the strident calls to tone it down, to find something that will appeal to 'modern man'. (I had two letters saying that just this last week.)

It can't be done. The women wouldn't have been so terrified if they'd merely had a new, heart-warming spiritual experience. They wouldn't have run away in panic just because, in their heart of hearts, they had suddenly come to believe that Jesus was somehow 'there' with them, that his cause would continue, that his teaching would stand the test of time. (All of these are things that people have said in the misguided effort to avoid what the New Testament writers are saying. But the word 'resurrection' simply doesn't, and didn't, mean any of those things.)

I take it more or less for granted, by the way, that verse 8 is not where Mark himself concluded his gospel. Look at the Dead Sea Scrolls (in the Israel Museum in Jerusalem, or in facsimile, online or elsewhere). A great many of them have lost the beginning and the end, or both. That stands to reason: the two ends of the scroll would be attached to sticks, and might easily have been torn off. If, instead of a scroll, a very early copy of Mark was bound up as a primitive book (a 'codex'), the same thing could happen to the sheets at either end. In any case, Mark certainly doesn't mean us to understand that the women *never* said anything to anybody, that they stayed silent for life. He must only mean that in their panic and fear they went straight back to the house where they were staying without telling any passers-by, or people they saw in the street, what was going on.

This account, in fact, reads like what it almost certainly is: a very, very early description of what happened that first Easter morning, told from one point of view, told (like all eyewitness accounts) quite selectively, with a few details tossed in with an almost breathless wonder. The stone! The young man! Going to Galilee! It made no sense then, and it barely makes sense now (we can see Mark saying), but this is the way they told the story and, once told, it's better to keep it as it is. Certainly we can contrast this quick, unadorned tale with the developed account of the crucifixion, where in the telling and retelling the early church has quite properly allowed all sorts of hints of scripture, and other shapings of the narrative, to come in. Here we have none of that.

Easter is meant to be a surprise. It is certainly not a 'happy ending' after the horror of the cross, though sadly some churches treat it like that. Mark 16 doesn't read like a 'happy ending'. It reads like a shocking new beginning – which of course is what Mark intends. The story is not over. In fact, it's just starting: the new story, the story which is now possible because Jesus has been enthroned as king of the Jews, as king of the world, as sovereign over death itself, as the one who is now going to do strange new things, surprising his closest friends and his most implacable enemies. A new way of living, a new way of being human, has been launched upon the world, a way that people thought impossible then and think impossible still today, but a way that has caught up millions and transformed their lives beyond recognition.

Easter Day is, of course, an event of cosmic significance. But, as always in the gospel, the large-scale meaning doesn't squeeze out the deeply personal implication. Notice the little mention in verse 7: 'go and tell his disciples – including Peter . . .'. Peter had, of course, let Jesus down badly. He boasted and blustered and then fell flat on his face. But Easter is all about new starts. That was true for Peter. It's true for us, too.

Today

Lord of life, risen from the dead, lead us on through fear and astonishment to share in the new work of your kingdom.

EASTER MONDAY

Mark 16.9–end

[9]When Jesus was raised, early on the first day of the week, he appeared first of all to Mary Magdalene, from whom he had cast out seven demons. [10]She went and told the people who had been with him, who were mourning and weeping. [11]When they heard that he was alive, and that he had been seen by her, they didn't believe it.

[12]After this he appeared in a different guise to two of them as they were walking into the countryside. [13]They came back and told the others, but they didn't believe them.

[14]Later Jesus appeared to the eleven themselves, as they were at table. He told them off for their unbelief and hardheartedness, for not believing those who had seen him after he had been raised.

[15]'Go into all the world,' he said to them, 'and announce the message to all creation. [16]Anyone who believes and is baptized will be rescued, but people who don't believe will be condemned. [17]And these signs will happen around those who believe: they will drive out demons in my name, they will speak with new tongues, [18]they will pick up serpents in their hands; and if they drink anything poisonous it won't harm them. They will lay their hands on the sick, and they will get better.'

> [19]When the Lord Jesus had spoken with them, he was taken up into heaven, and sat down at God's right hand. [20]They went out and announced the message everywhere. The Lord worked with them, validating their message by the signs that accompanied them.

When I became Dean of Lichfield in 1994, one of the first things I saw as I was shown around the magnificent cathedral was the place where the building had been, as it were, stitched back together again after the serious damage it had suffered during the Civil War three hundred and fifty or so years earlier. (The cathedral tower had been used, shamefully, as a post for snipers, so it had become a 'legitimate' target.) At first it seemed to me really sad that the building hadn't been mended, as it were, 'invisibly', in the way a tailor will mend a suit that's had a tear. Surely that would have been better, more honouring to God?

A moment's reflection made me think differently. Whether for good or ill, that cathedral had stood at the heart of England at one of the most appalling periods in our history. It had shared in the violence and destruction, and had come through to be, once more, a place of prayer, sanctuary and pilgrimage. The marks were still showing; but that wasn't a bad thing. That is how the church often is. That is how, according to Luke and John, Jesus himself was: risen from the dead, no longer to suffer pain, but recognizable by the mark of the nails. There is a profound truth there about the nature of the people of God.

Perhaps there is a profound truth there too about the nature of scripture. Mark's gospel, as I said, was most likely broken off at verse 8. Mark almost certainly wrote more than that, but we don't have his conclusion. Someone else – actually, at least two other people – have added the 'endings' we now have, the extra bit of verse 8 on the one hand and then verses 9–20 on the other. The marks still show. Scripture, the record of God's messy and damaging entry into his own world, is itself at this point rather obviously messy and damaged. That seems to make the point rather well.

Anyway, the key thing about this extra 'ending', which someone has written and which has found its way into some fairly early manuscripts, is the double sense – which of course we find in the other gospels, as well as in Acts – that Jesus is truly now the Lord of the whole world, and that he is sending out his followers to put that lordship into operation. A word about both of these is in order.

First, Jesus is indeed Lord. This is the main point of his resurrection, as the early formula in Romans 1.3–5 makes clear: the resurrection demonstrates that he always was the 'son of God', and has now been powerfully and publicly declared to be Israel's Messiah, the world's true king. The resurrection isn't about 'proving that there's a life after death' or 'showing that God still loves us' or any such thing. Those are true but, by comparison with the reality, they are trivial. Indeed, such interpretations can be, sadly, ways by which Christians have avoided the much sharper implications of the resurrection. The risen Jesus 'was taken up into heaven, and sat down at God's right hand'. The way this reads, it almost sounds like a physical description; but whoever wrote this passage was far more in tune with the key biblical texts than we are, and in this case we are surely meant to pick up the echoes of Jesus' answer to Caiaphas in 14.62. The 'son of man' has indeed 'come with the clouds of heaven' and is now 'sitting at the right hand of Power', as in Daniel 7.13 and Psalm 110.1.

The signs that this has indeed taken place in 'heaven' (heaven being God's space, interlocking and intersecting with our space and indeed taking charge of it) is that Jesus' followers, to this day, have been able to 'go into all the world' and 'announce the message to all creation'. We need to be clear at this point. As anyone who has tried to explain the gospel to an unbeliever knows only too well, announcing the message is neither easy nor straightforward. It isn't just that people find it incredible;

they find it both ridiculous (whoever heard of a crucified Jew being raised from the dead? And whoever would have thought of such a person being the lord of the world?) and offensive (if this catches on, I will have to give up a lot of things in my world-view and daily life that are central and important to me). But these surprised and unprepared messengers go out anyway, with no great skill of their own but simply with 'the message', the good news. And *the Lord worked with them*. That is the key. The sovereign power of the enthroned Jesus goes to work – Paul and other writers might add, 'through his spirit' – so that, when the message is announced, people's hearts are softened, and to their own great surprise they find that they believe it.

The messengers will also do other things, some of which appear startling in today's world, to say the least. Handling snakes and drinking poison may well be intended literally (as in Acts 28.3–6, where a snake fastens on to Paul but doesn't harm him), but might well be seen metaphorically as well (as Paul himself hints when he alludes to the idea of the snake in Romans 16.20). Casting out demons, speaking in new tongues, and healing the sick are all, of course, well attested in the early church. The point of them all is not so much to perform magic tricks to convince people that Jesus is alive and well, but rather to be signs and symbols of the healing work of the gospel going out into new countries, rescuing bodies and souls from the corrupt and corrupting powers that have enslaved them.

And if the church, in following this commission, still shows signs of its own muddle, brokenness, failing and sin – God can take care of that too. Obviously it would be better if none of these things were so. But the God who can call someone to fill in the missing bits of a very early gospel can stitch up the seams of our life and witness, too. All things are possible, Jesus had said, for those who believe. That remains at the heart of Mark's resurrection message.

Today

Give us your power, Almighty Lord, that we may bear faithful witness to your risen life.

EASTER TUESDAY

Mark 2.23–27

²³One sabbath, Jesus was walking through the cornfields. His disciples made their way along, plucking corn as they went.

²⁴'Look here,' said the Pharisees to him, 'why are they doing something illegal on the sabbath?'

²⁵'Haven't you ever read what David did,' replied Jesus, 'when he was in difficulties, and he and his men got hungry? ²⁶He went into God's house (this was when Abiathar was high priest), and ate the "bread of the presence", which only the priests were allowed to eat – and he gave it to the people with him.

²⁷'The sabbath was made for humans,' he said, 'not humans for the sabbath.'

I have often used, as an illustration, the way in which signposts work. A signpost tells you not where you are at the moment, but where you are going to. You don't put a sign (I have often said) saying 'This Way to London' in Piccadilly Circus, or 'This Way to New York' in Times Square. The point should be obvious: when you arrive at your destination, you don't need signposts any more.

Since moving to Scotland, I have discovered a striking exception to my rule. We live near the tiny village of Kilconquhar. Right in the centre of the village, near the church and opposite the pub, is a milestone telling you how far it is to various other towns. But at the top of the milestone, to my astonishment and amusement, it says, 'Kil'r 0'. No miles to Kilconquhar. Zero. You're there already. Was it a joke? Did someone put it there in case of very thick fog, in which case some muddled

179

travellers might be glad to know not just where they were going, but where they already were? It's hard to say.

The point about the sabbath controversies in the gospels, of which this is one of the most famous ones, is that for the Jews the sabbath wasn't simply a day of rest at the end of each week. The sabbath institution formed a great long line of signposts, from the earliest days of creation and covenant right on through, pointing forwards to the time when God would give 'rest' to his people once and for all. Sabbaths were markers on the road, signs pointing ahead.

And Jesus had come to announce that the time was fulfilled (1.15). That's why, as we recall, his disciples did not fast. They had stopped commemorating the sadnesses of the old world; they were celebrating the joys of the new one. They weren't putting up any more signposts, pointing away into the future; God's future had arrived in the present.

Easter is an especially good moment to consider this. Holy Saturday, the Jewish sabbath, was the time of preparation for the new creation that was about to burst forth. Once you have Easter Day, you can never go back to signposts. The old has gone, the new has arrived. That's why, of course, the earliest Christians met on Sundays (though they never spoke of this as a new sabbath; that would have made all the wrong points).

That is what lies underneath this discussion, and others like it. Some have objected that the Pharisees were a strict sect who would hardly spend their time hanging around Galilean cornfields on the off chance of finding people breaking the sabbath. But there are two answers to this. First, we know from some contemporary sources that there were many Pharisees who in fact did make it their business to police, unofficially but powerfully, the major symbols of Jewish identity. Second, today's self-appointed guardians of public morality (I mean journalists, of course) may well not go and wait with their long-lens cameras to catch ordinary mortals up to no good. But if someone is famous, royal, a celebrity – well, they will cross land and sea to take a single photograph. Jesus was acquiring a reputation as a reformer, and more than a reformer. There is every reason to suppose that people who valued strict observance of ancestral traditions would do their best to see whether he was keeping them or not.

As usual, there are other dimensions to the story as well. The claim of Jesus to be 'fulfilling the time' is part of his larger claim – made by implication here and all over the place – to be Israel's true king. As such, he's in an odd position, of course, since the present authorities don't see him like that. But Jesus refers them to a passage of scripture in which King David himself, who had already been anointed but had not yet been enthroned as king, was on the run from Saul. David was already sovereign over Israel's institutions, in this case the rules governing the holy Tabernacle (the forerunner of the Temple). Jesus was claiming that he was now sovereign over the institutions, too, partly because he was 'the son of man', Israel's representative, the one who would receive authority in the end (Daniel 7), and partly because, as such, he was ushering in the new day. The journey was over; the signposts were no longer needed. Easter is like that. Time to leave behind the old life, and launch out on the new one.

Today

Show us, Lord of all wisdom, where we are clinging to the old signposts when you are leading us forwards to the goal.

EASTER WEDNESDAY

Mark 4.26–33

²⁶'This is what God's kingdom is like,' said Jesus. 'Once upon a time a man sowed seed on the ground. ²⁷Every night he went to bed; every day he got up; and the seed sprouted and grew without him knowing how it did it. ²⁸The ground produces crops by itself: first the stalk, then the ear, then the complete

corn in the ear. ²⁹But when the crop is ready, in goes the sickle at once, because harvest has arrived.'

³⁰'What shall we say God's kingdom is like?' he said. 'What picture shall we give of it? ³¹It's like a grain of mustard seed. When it's sown on the ground, it's the smallest of all the seeds of the earth. ³²But when it's sown, it springs up and becomes the biggest of all shrubs. It grows large branches, so that "the birds of the air make their nests" within its shade.'

³³He used to tell them a lot of parables like this, speaking the word as much as they were able to hear.

Easter, in the northern hemisphere at least, is a time when all sorts of plants are starting to come up. Sometimes there are surprises. I well remember raising my eyebrows a few years ago when bulbs we had totally forgotten about appeared in places we hadn't expected them.

That, of course, is the point of the little parables of the kingdom here, towards the end of Mark 4. Jesus wasn't one to let a good source of imagery go to waste with only one or two variations. These parables, though making different points to the 'Sower' at the start of the chapter, are nevertheless, so to speak, planted in the same soil.

They are precisely Easter parables: parables of surprise, of seeds sown and coming up unexpectedly, of growth that nobody even understands. There is even an extra 'Easter' hint embedded within the first one. The man who's planted the seed goes to bed and gets up every day – for the early Christians, 'sleep' and 'waking' were a natural code for 'dying' and 'rising' – and the seed is doing the same thing, *but he doesn't know how*. It's as though there is a hidden truth there which is both very obvious and deeply mysterious. It's just like the deepest truth of Jesus' whole public career: he was planting seeds that would 'die' and then 'rise', and he himself would ultimately be the seed that would die and rise, and bear much fruit – even though the people of God then, and the world ever since, can't figure out what Jesus was all about. Much like the man going to bed and getting up again, in fact.

Within that again, there is a sense of surprise at a different level. Consider how the crop appears (verse 28). First the stalk, then the ear, then the complete corn in the ear. At the moment, Jesus is saying, there may not be very much to see. A wandering prophet or preacher, telling people that God's kingdom is arriving; a travelling healer, gathering crowds but not getting them organized into a military body to march on Jerusalem. That was what people saw going on. What was it supposed to be all about? What sort of a movement was this intended to be?

Well, comes the answer in the parable: when the crop is ready, in goes the sickle; harvest has arrived. Some have suggested that Jesus was hinting here, after all, at an eventual military coup. But this goes against everything else we know of him. Far more likely that he was using the image of harvest and sickle, granted their obvious Old Testament background (Joel 3.13), for the coming of God's kingdom. At present, he is saying, there are small shoots, but the time is coming when we shall reap a great harvest.

And yes: this again is a classic Easter message. New life is springing up. When a church is formed in this town, or that village, all people may see is a few folk going into a building on Sunday morning. They may think nothing more of it. But, if the church is truly planted, fairly soon there will be changes. In people's lives. In the community and the neighbourhood. And when one single person turns to God and allows the 'dying' to take place in their own life – when the seed is properly sown, in repentance, faith and baptism – then nobody can tell what astonishing fruit will come up.

That leads us on to the next parable, the mustard seed. Jesus is once again explaining that just because the kingdom-work which he is beginning seems to be starting very small that doesn't mean it isn't the real planting of a powerful seed. No doubt he faced challenges on this front in his own day ('How can this be God's kingdom? Just a wandering healer with some strange ideas?'), much as we are likely to in ours ('How can the church really be God's people? Just a bunch of fussy old folk muttering their prayers . . .?' or 'How can this person really claim to be a Christian? Just because they've given up getting drunk and started reading the Bible . . .?'). But if people were expecting large-scale mustard trees to appear fully grown, they haven't understood the way God works. Look back at Genesis 1. God has designed his world to work by means of seeds being sown, through the steady process of planting, tending and harvest.

Don't despise small things, then. Think back to the first Easter: a few scared women, a bunch of muddled and frightened disciples. Yet within a few weeks they were standing up to the authorities in Jerusalem; and within a century the Roman emperor was getting anxious letters about those Christians in northern Turkey. Easter is like that. The seed is sown in the dark earth, but when it comes up there's no knowing what it will do.

Today

Sow your word in our hearts and our lives, Lord of the harvest, so that in due time we may reap abundantly and celebrate your risen power at work.

EASTER THURSDAY

Mark 12.28–34

[28]One of the legal experts came up, and overheard the discussion. Realizing that Jesus had given a splendid answer, he put a question of his own.

'Which commandment', he asked, 'is the first one of all?'

[29]'The first one', replied Jesus, 'is this: "Listen, Israel: the Lord your God, the Lord is one; [30]and you shall love the Lord your God with all your heart, and with all your soul, and with

all your understanding, and with all your strength." [31]And this is the second one: "You shall love your neighbour as yourself." No other commandment is greater than these ones.'

[32]'Well said, Teacher,' answered the lawyer. 'You are right in saying that "he is one and there is no other beside him", [33]and that "to love him with all the heart, and with all the intelligence, and with all the strength" and "to love one's neighbour as one-self" is worth far more than all burnt offerings and sacrifices.'

[34]Jesus saw that his answer came out of deep understanding. 'You are not far from God's kingdom,' he said to him.

After that, nobody dared put any more questions to him.

As the Nazi party was increasing its power in pre-war Germany, the great theologian Karl Barth, still at that stage teaching in Bonn, came into contact one day with one of the party officials. The policies that had made the Nazis popular at that stage included the claim that they were pulling the country back from the anarchy and chaos of earlier years to 'law and order', tidying up society as it were and bringing it into shape.

'Don't you think, Herr Barth,' said the official, 'that what we need today is the Ten Commandments?'

'Yes,' replied Barth. 'Especially the first one.'

Barth saw through the pretence. The Nazis weren't really interested in morality at all. They wanted to put up a front of legal rectitude behind which they would smuggle in all their own agendas, enforcing them on a population that was becoming used to behaving properly, to allowing lawful authority to go unchallenged. But at the head of the Ten Commandments is the one that puts everything on a different plane: 'I am the Lord your God, who brought you out of the land of Egypt.' And if God is God, and if he claims our total and ultimate allegiance, then all the schemes and plots of the Nazis were called into question. Perhaps not surprisingly, Barth was soon forced out of Germany and went back to his native Switzerland.

Barth's theological (and political) instinct was, of course, fuelled by a lifetime of being soaked in the scriptures. And here, near the heart of Mark's account of Jesus' debates in Jerusalem in the days before his death, we find an exchange in which both Jesus and his questioner end up in agreement, and with Jesus saying the remarkable words, 'You are not far from God's kingdom.' What was it that the legal expert had grasped? How does this help us to see our way, as Easter people, into the work of that kingdom for ourselves?

Recall what's just happened. Here in Mark 12 Jesus is poised between two things: his dramatic action in the Temple in chapter 11, and the great and frightening discourse of chapter 13, focused on the Temple's upcoming destruction. Virtually all the material in chapters 11 and 12 deals, from one angle or another, with the question: what was Jesus saying about the Temple? What was he saying about the kingdom? How did it all work out?

Jesus' answer, by itself, was fairly unremarkable. The great rabbis would often debate questions like this. For Jesus to answer with the matchless 'Shema' prayer (Deuteronomy 6.4–5), 'Hear, O Israel: the LORD our God, the LORD is one' (NIV), with its command to love God with every fibre of one's being – and then to append 'love your neighbour as yourself' (which comes from Leviticus 19.18) – all this, though powerful, might have been seen as quite a 'safe' answer.

But the legal expert, still no doubt pondering what Jesus had done in the Temple, goes one little but all-important step further. *If you really love God and your neighbour like that,* he ponders, *you won't need the sacrificial system at all, will you?*

Mark doesn't say that Jesus smiled, but if you were producing this passage as a mini-play you would certainly get the actor to do just that. The 'deep understanding' that the legal expert had displayed was exactly in line with the 'deep understanding' of Jesus himself about the whole purpose of his mission. Like the sabbath (a signpost pointing forward to the great 'rest', the restoration of the whole creation); like the food laws, designed to keep Israel 'pure' until the time when purity of heart was at last to be attainable; so the Temple itself, the building where heaven and earth met, and where the regular sacrifices kept God and Israel in communion, *was designed by God as a temporary symbol until the ultimate reality arrived.* The whole point of Jesus' kingdom-proclamation was that the time of waiting was over. 'The time is fulfilled!' (1.15). Jesus is now offering, to anybody and everybody who will hear and believe, the reality to which the Temple itself was a signpost. As in chapters 7 and 10, so here, it appears that he sees 'the kingdom of God' as the new reality in which those who believe will indeed love God with all their hearts, and their neighbours as themselves. And to do this they won't need the Temple. He has, in effect, declared it redundant: not because it was a silly idea in the first place, but because the reality to which it pointed has now arrived.

We may well think, even as we celebrate Easter, that we still have a long way to go before we have, ourselves, arrived at the kind of life that Jesus assumes his people will live. But the point is not that we suddenly become completely perfect. The point is that the way is open, for anyone who takes Jesus seriously, to know and experience that mutual love with God that is the hallmark of all serious Christian faith, and to offer, to everybody we meet, that outgoing, creative, healing love that Jesus himself offered to all and sundry. If Jesus is truly risen from the dead, nothing – even the renewal and transformation of the human heart! – is now impossible.

Today

Give us, loving Lord, such love for you, and for one another, that our lives may display your glory to the world of hate and fear.

EASTER FRIDAY
Mark 12.41–44

[41]As he sat opposite the Temple treasury, he watched the crowd putting money into the almsboxes. Lots of rich people put in

substantial amounts. [42]Then there came a single poor widow, who put in two tiny coins, together worth a single penny.

[43]Jesus called his disciples.

'I'm telling you the truth,' he said. 'This poor widow just put more into the treasury than everybody else. [44]You see, all the others were contributing out of their wealth; but she put in everything she had, out of her poverty. It was her whole livelihood.'

The old ones are the best. 'I was on a plane,' said the comedian Bob Hope, 'and suddenly it started to go into a spin and head straight for earth. Everybody was panicking and someone said, "Do something religious!"'

'So,' he said, 'I took up a collection.'

We smile, because the stereotype is all too familiar. I was in a church the other day where we had a regular offering, and then, because there was some special event coming up, there was a second offering specially for that; then, as we left church, there was someone standing at the door with a plate for yet another good cause, just in case anyone had any spare change left in their pockets or handbags. It did not, shall we say, create a good impression. In fact I do not now remember anything else at all about that service.

Now, of course the church has to pay its way. If people don't give to support mission, ministry and the buildings where they happen, the doors will soon be shut. And we all know that 'God loves a cheerful giver' (2 Corinthians 9.7). So do we, if it comes to that. Generosity – when it obviously comes from the heart – is a lovely and loveable thing, not simply when we happen to be the recipients.

But money is always good for a wry smile, whether the subject is income tax, bankers' bonuses, mortgage rates, or anything else. In my country at least, we all find it slightly embarrassing. And, as a result, many clergy go in the opposite direction to the one who organized that triple collection. We don't want to put people off, so we don't mention it.

But one of the little-known facts of the human anatomy is that there is a direct electronic link between two key organs: the heart and the wallet. Actually, and interestingly, the link seems to work in both directions. Of course, someone whose heart has been warmed and transformed by the preaching and living of the gospel will be only too ready to share what they have with the community, the pastor(s) and the teacher(s) through whom they have come to enjoy that transformation and the fellowship that it brings. But, equally, there are many people who have given to God's work more from a sense of social or civic duty (when a large local church has a special appeal, say) and who, to their surprise and perhaps alarm, find that they are thereupon drawn in and, themselves, transformed.

In this case, of course, the former link seems to be working better than the latter. The rich people are putting money into the treasury almost as a way of holding it (and the Temple which it supports) at arm's length. ('We've done our bit,' you can sense them thinking, 'so now we won't have to worry about all that stuff for a while.') But the widow, putting in two tiny coins, is clearly overflowing with love for God. And, as we know in theory but often forget in practice, what counts is not the amount but the proportion. The rich put in large sums but a small percentage; she put in a tiny sum but the maximum percentage. She was prepared to go without, for herself, rather than stint on giving what she could to God.

As a result, of course, she becomes a parade example of that total love for God of which Jesus was speaking earlier in the chapter. This is the last incident before the great discourse in which Jesus predicts the destruction of the Temple, and it's almost as though Mark has placed it here to say to us that the reality to which the Temple points is alive and well, even in this poor widow. There is such a thing as a total love for God, and it will show up in your giving.

This in turn comes through into the life of the Easter people as we see it in Acts and in Paul's letters. Once God's new creation has arrived, God's people can rely on his provision for all their needs; and part of that provision will be in the pockets of their better-off Christian neighbours. The early church lived as a *family*, a family where the needs of the one would be met directly by the generosity of the other. They were in it together. And this affects the very meaning of the word 'love' itself. When Paul tells the Thessalonians that they already love one another and that he wants them to do so more and more (1 Thessalonians 4.9–10) he doesn't just mean that they should have nice, warm feelings for one another. 'Love' here means 'charitable concern', 'mutual support' or something like that. I suspect that if members of Paul's churches were to be miraculously transplanted into one of today's Western churches, among the things that would horrify them would be the way in which the vast majority of Christians retreat, when it comes to money, into their own nuclear families and special-interest zones. Of course, our knowledge of the worldwide church and the severe needs suffered by many of our brothers and sisters there is now almost too full: we can't take it all in, and we certainly don't think we can do anything about it. We're right; by ourselves, we can't. But if God's people as a whole took the story of the widow's two coins seriously (and linked them, as Mark fairly obviously links them, with the challenge to love God and our neighbour), it would be surprising just what a difference it could make.

Today

Give us generous hearts, good Lord, that we may show our love for you and for one another in response to all your love for us.

EASTER SATURDAY

John 20.19–31

[19]On the evening of that day, the first day of the week, the doors were shut where the disciples were, for fear of the Judaeans. Jesus came and stood in the middle of them.

'Peace be with you,' he said. [20]With these words, he showed them his hands and his side. Then the disciples were overjoyed when they saw the master.

[21]'Peace be with you,' Jesus said to them again. 'As the father has sent me, so I'm sending you.'

[22]With that, he breathed on them.

'Receive the holy spirit,' he said. [23]'If you forgive anyone's sins, they are forgiven. If you retain anyone's sins, they are retained.'

[24]One of the Twelve, Thomas (also known as Didymus), wasn't with them when Jesus came. [25]So the other disciples spoke to him.

'We've seen the master!' they said.

'Unless I see the mark of the nails in his hands,' replied Thomas, 'and put my finger into the nail-marks, and put my hand into his side – I'm not going to believe!'

[26]A week later the disciples were again in the house, and Thomas was with them. The doors were shut. Jesus came and stood in the middle of them.

'Peace be with you!' he said.

[27]Then he addressed Thomas.

'Bring your finger here', he said, 'and inspect my hands. Bring your hand here and put it into my side. Don't be faithless! Just believe!'

[28]'My Lord,' replied Thomas, 'and my God!'

[29]'Is it because you've seen me that you believe?' replied Jesus. 'God's blessing on people who don't see, and yet believe!'

[30]Jesus did many other signs in the presence of his disciples, which aren't written in this book. [31]But these ones are written so that you may believe that the Messiah, the son of God, is none other than Jesus; and that, with this faith, you may have life in his name.

One of the most popular misconceptions today is the idea that everybody up to about two centuries ago was credulous, gullible, easily taken in by strange stories and odd beliefs. We, however, with our modern 'scientific' knowledge, have learnt how to be sceptical, to test everything, not to take odd stories on trust but to enquire for ourselves. And so on.

There are a million counter-examples, of course (not least the many contemporary stories of people who are duped by the fantasies of politicians, economists and the like); but among the most obvious is this wonderful story of Thomas. Thomas knew perfectly well that dead people don't rise. He knew, only too well, that there had been many would-be 'messiahs' and 'prophets' in recent memory, and that, one by one, they had been killed off by the authorities, or even by rival gangs. And that had been the end of that. No point pretending you could carry on when you obviously couldn't.

Thomas wanted to see, and to touch. The evidence of the senses is a wonderful thing. As the story goes on, of course, Jesus gently points out that it would have been better to have believed without seeing; John is recording this for the benefit of his own readers, who have not had, as he has had, the privilege of intimate human contact with 'the Word of Life' (1 John 1.1). But Jesus does not (as some of today's apologists might have told him to do) refuse Thomas's grumpy request. The story of Thomas, in fact, shows something which we see in John's gospel in scene after scene, as those vivid one-to-one encounters unfold: Jesus and Nicodemus, Jesus and the woman at the well, Jesus and the man by the pool, Jesus and the man born blind, even Jesus and Pilate. On each occasion, no doubt, Jesus could have taken the high moral ground and simply refused to address the questions he was being asked. (The closest we get to that is the interview with Pilate, but there are all sorts of other things going on there as well.) But, instead, he meets his puzzled questioner where he, or she, is. And that is what happens here, too.

But then the miracle occurs. Thomas has said he wants not only to see, but to touch. Very well, says Jesus, 'Bring your finger here, and inspect my hands. Bring your hand here and put it into my side.' That's what Thomas has asked for; that's what Jesus will offer him.

But we are not told (despite a long tradition of Christian art, in which Thomas does indeed reach out his hand and touch Jesus) that Thomas obeys. Instead, he simply says the words, the words which bring into speech the confession of faith which had been trembling on the edge of so many conversations earlier in the book but which now at last comes blurting out: 'My Lord and my God!' *The Word became flesh*, said John at the start, *and we gazed upon his glory*. In the risen Jesus, recognized by the mark of the nails, the wounds of love, that glory is fully revealed, and Thomas leapfrogs over all the others, from radical doubt to robust faith. And this, says John, is the faith for which his whole book was written. The Jewish people had been waiting for the Messiah, but not at all sure what he would look like or what he would do. Now, he says, we know. 'The Messiah, the son of God, is none other than Jesus.' This is the faith in which life is to be found, the 'life' that is God's new life, the life of God's new age, the different dimension of life that can be born inside us here and now and will go on for ever and ever, all the way through death and to our own resurrection at the last.

It is because of this faith, which has always seemed impossible to sceptics but which is in fact within reach of anyone at all, that Jesus sends the disciples out on their mission. 'As the father has sent me,' he said (verse 21), 'so I'm sending you.' That is the most breathtaking commission and responsibility we could imagine. In that *As . . . so . . .* there lies the secret of all Christian mission. Think back, all through the Lenten journey, to all that we have seen and learnt of Jesus. Remember, incident by incident, what he was doing, announcing God's kingdom and making it happen wherever he went, bringing healing and hope, food for the hungry and wisdom for the foolish. Now ask yourself: what would it take for us to do that, to *be* that, for our world today and tomorrow? Answer that question, and you have found the key to Christian mission.

But, you say, that's absurd! Jesus was Jesus; we are weak, frail, muddled humans. We're going to get it wrong. And even if we get it right, sometimes, it won't work. Nothing will happen. But the truth of Easter is not just that Jesus himself was raised from the dead by the power of God. The truth of Easter is that that same power is now unleashed into the lives of all who believe in Jesus, all who follow him, so that *he* can continue *his* work – through them. Jesus breathed on them, like God himself breathing on the first human pair in Genesis 2.7, and that breath of life sent his followers out into the world then and does so still today.

We go out, then, as Easter people, with the message both of forgiveness and warning, of faith that confronts and conquers doubt, and of hope that overcomes fear (verse 19). We go out, in fact, as people of new creation: John emphasizes in verse 19, as he had done in the first verse of the chapter, that this was 'the first day of the week'. It was the beginning of God's new world. We new-creation people are to fill our lungs with Jesus' powerful breath, to fill our minds with the truth of his resurrection, to fill our hearts with love for him and his world, and to go out, not knowing where we shall go or what we shall do, but only that a new day has begun which will never end. We are to remind ourselves, again and again, that the love which was shown on the cross (revealed once more here in the mark of the nails, verse 20) is the same powerful love that will carry us forward, through all the suffering and sorrow that we too will meet, to the point where not only we, but a great company that nobody could count, will say 'My Lord and my God'. There are, as John says, many other things that he could have written in this book. But this is enough: enough for us, and for the world, to believe, to find life. Easter life. Here and now.

194

Today

Lord Jesus, King and Master; overcome our fears with your love, and our doubts with your life, so that we may take that love and life to the ends of the world.